Crawfish Jesse

A Soldier's Diary 1893 -1918

Alison M. Wilkom

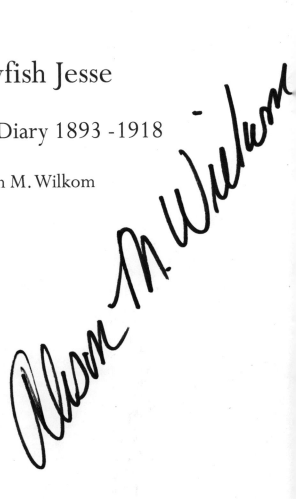

ISBN: 1-4392-5707-8
ISBN-13: 9781439257074

Dedication

For the masses of people who thirst for something new. To my family, words can never say how much I love you all. I know I drove you nuts over the years. To My friends who have supported me during my ups and downs. My father also dedicates this book to his father. Lastly to Jesse who died a warrior. Ride Em' boys, Ride Em'!

Book of Contents

Captain Dodd's Monkey Drill

Jesse's diary may not be reproduced in any manner whatsoever
without written permission.

Prologue

This book is a result of a diary written by my father's grandfather who was Jesse C. Davisson, John R. Day and Henry C. Hays. These are the names he used whilst serving in the United States Cavalry, and other branches of the U.S. Army. His real name is Jesse C. Davisson. It was never unusual to use different names while serving in the Army. First Sergeants were known to say during roll call, "Now boys remember your Army name." Jesse compiled his diary in 1940 when he was confined to bed. A chest problem arose from chemical warfare gassings in France, during WW1.

According to Jesse he was born 17 January 1868 in Philadelphia, Pennsylvania. Jesse married a woman from Philadelphia who was my father's grandmother. The couple took up residency with Jesse's mother. They lived in a section of Philadelphia known as Fairmont Park at 33rd and Diamond Streets. His wife's family was from a section of the city known as Fishtown. Fishtown is approximately thirty-five city blocks from 33rd and Diamond Streets. Jesse's mother controlled the purse strings, and made life difficult for the new couple. Jesse's mother was so stingy with her money that she would not give Jesse's wife, five cents for the trolley car ride to Fishtown. Jesse was catching hell from his wife and mother. So to solve the problem he went off and joined the Army.

At the Fairmount Recruiting Station on Fairmount Avenue Jesse was turned away because of his feet. As he was leaving a Sergeant told him to cross the Delaware into Camden, New Jersey and join there. Therefore that is what he did and was signed up for the Army on 26 January 1893. It was then he gave his first alias name. You will soon read in the book that Jesse went by a few names and wore many hats during his life. Follow him through his military timeline. Starting out and being placed in the 7th Cavalry not knowing how to ride a horse to well. He soon learned to ride. Horses became his best friends. Throw in some Indian Scouts and his fellow Horse Soldiers too. Jesse survived many ambushes, skirmishes, dodged bullets, avoided snakebites and local creepy crawlies on the cowboy trails. Find out why Jesse was one of the first Horse Soldiers to ever ride through the Black Mountains in Arizona.

During the Spanish War, Jesse survived the accident of the U.S. Transport Massachusetts. That had crashed onto a coral reef off the coast of Porto Rico, August 3 1898. Hid in the Philippine jungles from guerrillas with Bolo knifes ready to slit you throat. Saw and investigated the aftermath of the "Massacre of the 9th Infantry Regiment." Also known as: "Balangia Massacre", and "Balangia Affair." Jesse at that time was serving a tour of duty on Samar, and surrounding islands during the Boxer Rebellion. Jesse was also a part of the Expeditionary Forces (AEF) during WW1 in France 1918: Belleau Woods, Chateau Thierry, and Battle of Aisne-Marne*defensive Sector, where Jesse received the Victory Medal. Jesse saw service in the following wars: American Indian (Cowboy and Indians Cattle King era), Spanish War, Philippines, and WW1 in France.

It is amazing that Jesse was not injured or killed throughout his travels around the world. May you find Jesse's life as fascinating as I have! Learn about the hard life on the trail while **Jesse was a Muleskinner. Follow him throughout the book and imagine yourself riding alongside him** on the next adventure. Travel back in time when this country was not a nation but staked claims and territories. Read about Apache Indian Scouts whom he rode along and worked with. Stories of Cattle rustlers, thieves, murderers, outlaws including deserters, as Jesse once was. Read about saloons, women of the night, Mexican Banditos and Yaqui Indians. Read about Cibique Creek where an Indian Chef was killed. That's the day Jesse almost met his maker.

Descriptions of Jesse's medals are described at the time of receivership. Some designs may have changed. Other than Jesse's diary, the rest of the book is public information. This book contains material that may not be suitable for some. His diary tells of brutal killings and methods of torture. Hey, who wants all the sugarcoated things to read anyways? Enjoy!

Chapter 1

My feet St. Louis, my feet

I often thought about going into the Army. So one day I made up my mind to go. I went to the Recruiting Station Office on Fairmount Avenue in Philadelphia to join up. I was turned down because of my feet. One of the sergeants in the office told me to go to Camden, New Jersey and try to join up there. Well that is what I did. I joined the Army on 26 January 1893. There was me and six other fellows sworn in the same day.

We were given our uniforms. Boy we were proud of those uniforms. A blue uniform with a nice warm overcoat, a blue cape lined with yellow. That you would throw back over your shoulder. We would be sent to Jefferson Barracks, St Louis, Missouri.

We got on a train in Philadelphia and off we went on a thirteen hundred mile trip to St. Louis. On the way out we all agreed we wanted to see the cave where the outlaw Jesse James and his gang used to hideout. We got to Jefferson Barracks and was placed in a big room to sleep for the night.

Well about six in the morning a sergeant came in and shouted, "Fall out and police up the area." We said, "What the hell does fall out and police up the area mean?" The sergeant shouted, "You will soon find out." Sure enough we did. We had to go outside and pick up all the little pieces of paper, cigar, and cigarette butts. And just about everything else that did not move. Well after we policed up the area we went to breakfast. After breakfast we were told to go back to the big room (barracks) and fall in. Fall in means everybody gets together in a line real quick. Soon we were marched to another building, where we were given some more uniforms. A Carbine Rifle, a pistol, and a sabre. Then we were told to fall in at the barracks.

A sergeant walked up to us and said, "When you hear the bugler blow a call. You fall out with your stable clothes on." Now fall out means this. If you are in a building and told to fall out, you are really falling in outside. If you are outside and told to fall out, it means you are dismissed. If you are outside, you can only fall out. But if you are inside, you fall out to fall in. No wonder the damn government is so messed up they cannot even tell a man where to stand without making it complicated. The sergeant then said, "When you fall out be wearing your white stable clothes."   Well pretty soon the bugler made some kind of noise and we fell out to fall in. The stable clothes were like a pair of white overalls. Anyway we fell out and fell in, and were marched to the stables. Another sergeant walked over to us and shouted, "Fall out and stand to heel." Now in this case fall out meant we were suppose to go somewhere to fall in. But we did not know what stand to heel meant. We were all standing around looking at one another when the sergeant yelled, "Stand behind a horse." Then we were told to groom the horse. I groomed the horse for two hours, damn horse was a lot cleaner than I was. Then the sergeant yelled, "Fall out stand to heel facing your horse." Well this time we were a little quicker, and had some idea of what he meant. That is all we did the rest of the day fall in, fall out, fall in, fall out. The next day bright and early we again picked up all the little things off the ground.

Chapter 2
Feeling like a big shot

One day was a special day. This day we were going to actually ride a horse. We were told to get a set of reigns, and a blanket. And stand by your horse. The sergeant showed us how to put on the blankets and reins. After that the sergeant shouted, "Mount up." Well I have never seen such a thing in my life. Here we were us city boys trying to jump on a horse. People were falling all over the place cursing and what have.

The place we rode the horses was called the bullring. Finally the sergeant got tired of watching us and shouted, "Help one another up on a horse, and I will help the last man up." Well that is what we did. And soon we were all sitting up on a horse. I was feeling like a big shot. The sergeant said, "We will have a nice easy walk but not for long."

The next thing I knew the horse instead of walking is now going at a trot. You see the horses we rode knew the routine backwards and forwards. These horses would watch the sergeant's horse. And when the sergeant's horse started to go faster, your horse would go faster.

When your horse starts to trot you start moving from side to side. One man yelled, "Sergeant if you don't stop I will fall off!" "And you damn well will get back on!" yelled the sergeant. He no sooner said that when two fellows hit the ground. Let me tell you it is damn hard riding a horse with nothing under you but a blanket.

You are riding single file. And pretty soon the man in front of you starts weaving from side to side. The next thing you know you are doing the same thing. In a short time you fall off the horse. I took many a flop on old mother earth in them days of learning to ride.

It is bad enough riding the old horse and falling off. But the stable clothes got hot and sweaty. They would ride up your legs, and soon your legs were red and raw. Your backside hurts and you cannot sit down without pain. It even hurts to walk. We did this drill for three months along with a carbine pistol and sabre drill. The rest of your training you get when you get to your new post.

At Jefferson Barracks we had plenty to eat but only one blanket. You get a second blanket at your next post. It got cold at night in St Louis. And someone was detailed to keep a fire going in the old potbellied stove. Between this man throwing wood on the fire all night long, men snoring, and talking, you did not get a good night's rest. The three months I spent at Jefferson Barracks seemed like three years. One day it was over. I was going to a new outfit, Camp J.D. Mann in Texas.

Chapter 3

Lizards, Horned Toads, and Scorpions

Early one morning I was on a train heading for Laredo, Texas. We had a nice ride down on the train. A little drinking, a little gambling, and free eats supplied by the government. When I got off the train in Laredo I could hear some cowboys saying, "Some more tender meat for you sergeant." "Yeah." replied the sergeant. Who was there to pick us up. "Going to send them down to Camp J.D. Mann." said the sergeant. "Yes Sir! Camp J.D. Mann down on the Rio Grande." said the sergeant with a smile on his face.

We soon had our baggage off the train, and waited for the sergeant. He said, "Here is your special train that is going to take you down the Rio Grande." The sergeant was pointing to a big covered wagon. Hitched up to the wagon were six mules. And sitting in the driver's seat was one of the toughest looking characters I have ever seen. The wagon was called the Prairie Schooner. And the driver was known as a Jerk Line Driver.

We got our gear loaded it on the wagon, and started out. It was a damn rough ride in this wagon. Every time we hit a bump it would shake your guts out. On the way down the driver pointed out some of the local folks. Lizards, horned toads, scorpions, tarantula spiders, rattlesnakes, and lord knows what else.

When we camped for the night I kept thinking about all the local folk I had seen on the way down. We had some lunch left over from the train trip, and that is what we had for our supper. It was dark but no one was ready for sleep. We were all talking and thinking about snakes and what have you that we saw on the trail. The driver said, "Boys you better turn in now." Turn in hell! Then he shouted, "What the hell are you sitting around and looking at one another for? Do you think someone is going to give you a featherbed? You have seen the last of a featherbed for a long time. Your bed is here on the ground, and the sky is your roof." Somehow we got to sleep that night. But it was not easy.

Chapter 4

Jerk Line Drivers glee

In the morning we were looking for some wood to cook our breakfast with. The Jerk Line Driver shouted, "What the hell are you looking for?" "Wood to make a fire with." somebody said. "Wood hell!" shouted the Jerk Line Driver. "Get out there and pick up some buffalo chips." The

driver looked at us with our dumb expressions on our face and said, "You boys don't know what buffalo chips are? Come over here and I will show you. See that pile of dried cow shit? Well up among the Sioux Indians they call them buffalo chips. The Sioux have buffaloes down here we do not have any buffaloes. So we use dried cow shit from a Longhorn Steer. And you would soon find out what a Longhorn Steer is if he jabs you in the ass. Now pick up some buffalo chips! And cook your breakfast over them!" I must admit that is the first time I have ever had my breakfast cooked over a fire like that.

We soon started out after breakfast when all of a sudden the driver yelled, "Look at the big fellow over there!" I looked in the direction he was pointing. But I could not see anything. "Jesus you men are all blind!" he shouted. He jumped off the wagon with his big whip in his hand. All of a sudden, he let loose with the whip, and hit a big rattlesnake. It looked as big as a railroad tie. The snake jumped, we jumped, and the driver laughed. If I was to ever met the devil and he laughed, I know it would sound the same as the Jerk Line Drivers' glee. Everyone started running around and bumping into one another. The driver took out his pistol and shot the snake. He cut off its tail which had eleven rattlers on it and said, "Who wants the hide?" By this time we were all back on the wagon ready to go. He gave the rattlers to me. Many times since I have ridden by a snake, and did not know it was there. But your horse knew, and would start acting up.

Well we started out again with the scenery, and looking at the local folk creeping, crawling, hopping, and slithering along. As we were riding along the driver turned around and said, "Boys how would you like to wake up in the morning and find one of those big rattlers curled up on your chest?" How do you think we felt after that!

We stopped for the night. Cooked our supper over Sioux Wood, and settled down for the evening. Needless to say we were all thinking about what the driver said earlier. One of the fellows was out gathering some buffalo chips. When another fellow sneaked up on him, and grabbed him by the leg. This fellow started jumping around and shouting, "Son of a bitch, Son of a bitch!" He turned around and saw the man who grabbed him. "If I had a pistol I would shoot you right now!"

You see in addition to not getting a second blanket until you got to your next post. You did not get your weapons either. And that was lucky for one man that night. To start a fight that all you had to do was to reach over and grab someone when they were not looking.

The old driver stirred things up when he said, "Boys if a snake crawls up on your blanket during the night. Just let him lay there until morning and he will crawl off." "You old crazy Son of a bitch! Do you think I am going to lay there all night with a snake on my chest?" Someone shouted. "Well what would you do?" asked the driver. One man said, "I would pick up a brick, or a piece of lumber, and hit the snake." Well I thought to myself, that makes a lot of sense. The nearest lumber or brick yard, is probably thirty or forty miles away from here. Out here is nothing but sand, rocks, and mesquite wood. The mesquite is no good for burning, as you had to dig out the root. That is the only part that will burn. One of the fellows said, "Driver you are so damn smart! What would you do? If you woke up with a snake curled up on your chest?" The old driver looked around at all of us real slow like and said, "Why I would just reach down grab him, and bite off his head!" I knew that driver was a rough customer the first time I saw him. And, I believed he could have done just that.

The wind started kicking up a little bit so we decided to turn in for the night. The wind started blowing the tumbleweeds around. When all of a sudden, one man jumped up and started hollering, "Snakes got me! Snakes got me!" Seems the wind blew his blanket up around him, and some of the tumbleweed hit his blanket. He thought it was a snake. I am quite sure there was a few of us who thought as I did. If I had a pistol, I would shoot that Son of a bitch. For waking me up, and getting me all worried again. Now I am laying there thinking about snakes, lizards, horned toads, and everything else I had seen on the way down. One of the men named Tommy shouted at the driver, "You are the cause of this! You have us half scared to death with your talk about snakes on your chest upsetting everybody!" The old driver just laughed and said, "Didn't you want to be a Wild West Boy? You ought to be at home with your mother, sucking on a little bottle." Well we pulled through the night, but it was a long one. Next morning it was the same old thing. Buffalo chip round up, cook breakfast, load the wagon, and off we go to Camp J.D. Mann. On the way down hardly anyone said a word. Guess we were all wrapped up in our own thoughts.

Chapter 5
Arrival at Camp J.D. Mann

We arrived at the camp, and me and seven other fellows were assigned to the cavalry. I do not know where the others went. There were about twelve others if I remember right. A sergeant told us to get washed up and go eat. We looked around for a place to wash up in. The sergeant asked, "What the hell are you standing around for?" We said, "Where is the wash house?" "Wash house hell!" he shouted. "Get yourself down to the Rio Grande. And get washed there." So I got washed in the Rio Grande. Then went and got something to eat. Out there they hauled in the water for drinking. It was hauled in by some Mexicans by a mule train.

That night we had to make our own bed. We got some wood from a woodpile, some bailing wire, two blankets, and some hay. That is what I made my bed out of. We asked the sergeant if it was ok for us to sleep by the river, he said ok. Well me and Tommy set up our beds down by the river. Tommy was the fellow who shouted at the Jerk line Driver the night the driver said he would bite the snakes head off. As we were getting ready to go to sleep Tommy said, "Jess that old Jerk line Driver scared the hell out of me with his talking about snakes." We both must have been thinking the same thing, as we both jumped up and ran back to find the sergeant. We asked the sergeant if there were any snakes around. He said, "No. Too many people around here no snakes." That made Tommy and me feel a lot better. We went back down to the river. Most of the other soldiers were sleeping on the ground. Some were sleeping in a lean type of affair they made with the brush hauled up from the river.

Well Tommy and me settled down for the night, and went to sleep. All at once, I felt a sharp tug on my blanket. Only the tug was coming from underneath me. I was half-awake and turning over when Tommy said, "Jess why the hell are you pulling out the hay from underneath me?" Then I felt something pulling under me again. I looked up a little to the rear and was staring into the eyes of something very big. Well I jumped up, and Tommy jumped up. We went running, tripping over bodies, and shouting. I cannot remember what we were shouting. But we woke up the whole camp. Come to find out Tommy and me camped near a corral, where some Longhorn Steer were kept. And during the night the steers were eating our beds out from underneath us. Next night Tommy and me stayed close to the others.

Chapter 6

A gun, Two Texas Rangers, and mescal

One morning after breakfast we were called together, and told to get ready for horse drill. This drill was easier then the drill we had at Jefferson Barracks. Down here you learned to ride your horse all on your own. Plus we had a saddle. After three months of horse drill, I was a good saddler. We were told riding will come to you. And it did.

Soon I was assigned duty on the Rio Grande. I was told to keep a sharp lookout for Yaqui Indians also cattle rustlers, and smugglers. Jesus! I was worried about snakes, lizards, and Longhorn Cattle. Now I had to worry about Yaqui Indians, cattle rustlers, and smugglers. I would not know a Yaqui Indian if he walked up to me.

Let me tell you I was very scared out there in the dark hearing all kind of noises. As far as I was concerned someone could have smuggled all of Mexico over to where I was posted. All of a sudden, I heard a horse coming down the trail. I shouted, "Who goes there!" "Corporal of the Guard." was the reply. Oh Christmas was I happy. The Corporal of the Guard rode up and said, "How was your first tour of the guard duty?" To tell the truth I was kind of scared, and told the Corporal so. "I am scared out here, and still am. I could be killed out here. And no one would ever know about it." "Don't be stupid!" said the Corporal. "We have men all around you. There are men below you, and five Texas Rangers above you. Do you think we would be so stupid as to turn some greenhorn loose on his own out here?" After he told me that, I felt much better when I was on guard duty.

After a little while of serving guard duty I was turned out for duty with the old timers, and the Texas Rangers. We would wade across the Rio Grande into Mexico. And buy some mescal usually by the gallon. Drinking mescal was like drinking liquid fire. It is made from the cactus that grows out here.

There is a story about drinking mescal. A Texas Ranger had a gallon of it. He pointed his pistol at another Ranger and said, "Now take a drink of this." The other Ranger did and said, "This stuff is awful! How the hell can you stand to drink this stuff?" The Ranger holding the pistol said, "I know it is awful stuff. Now hold the pistol on me. And make me take a drink."

Chapter 7
Know how to skin a Rattler?

Where I was on the Rio Grande was very shallow and you could wade across to Mexico. While I was there we had some trouble with the Yaqui Indians. The Yaqui are a cross between a Mexican and an Indian. They were running cattle back and forth across the borders. They would steal only a few cattle at a time at night. Cattle do not like traveling at night, and do not like going through water at night. So they only stole a few at a time in order to control them. The Yaqui were tough customers. But if you treated them decent they did not give you much trouble. Treat them mean and you could end up with your throat slit.

One day me and nine other Calvary Men, three Indian Scouts, and four Texas Rangers were sent out. To see if we could find out who was rustling cattle from the Flying X Ranch. We were gone about twelve days on this trip. On the trail one of the Rangers killed a big rattlesnake. He asked me, "Do you know how to skin a rattler?" "No." I replied, "And I do not care to. I am scared to death of snakes." "You just getting broke in out here are you?" he asked. "Yes." I said. "An old Jerk Line Driver made me afraid of these snakes."

The other fellows dropped their reins and were lying on the ground talking. I asked the Ranger what he was going to do with the snake's skin. "Probably make a belt out of it. Or plaster it to my saddle." Then he said, "Tell you what I am going to do for you. Take my lariat. And when you go to sleep tonight, circle the lariat around the area you will be sleeping in. A snake will not cross a hair rope." I found out later this is what all the old timers do out here.

Soon we were off again looking for rustlers. One of the Indians told the Ranger he had found a freshly dug hole. We dug down and found parts of a dead steer. One of the Rangers said, "This is the work of Indians." The old Indian

Scout said, "Not the work of an Indian, but a white man." The Ranger got very angry over this statement. I thought he was going to hit the old scout. But he did not.

The Scout said, "Steer still has all its sinews. Indians will not leave sinews." "What he means" said one of the Rangers. "An Indian has use for sinews. For making clothing or what have you, and would always cut out the sinews to be used later." We kept looking but did not see any rustlers. So we headed back to camp.

On the way back we came across some Indians with a herd of sheep. We found out the sheep belonged to the Indians, but we had to chase them off the Flying X Ranch land. You see cattle will not graze where sheep have been. Some sheep clip the grass short and make a mess all over. So cattle stay away from the land sheep have been on. Soon we were back at camp. This was a big part of my life, day in day out, going out looking for cattle rustlers or guarding the border.

Chapter 8

Twenty shots pumped into him

This is a true story as it happened in the camp I was at. A man named Jake Sharp was sleeping in a tent. First call out in the morning was at six. Sometimes the bugler blew morning call, and sometimes he did not. Old Jake woke up. He stretched his arms, and felt something nice and soft on his chest. It did not take Jake too long to figure out what it was. He gave one big yell and jumped up. It was a damn big rattler, seventeen rattles on his tail. It was said the snake had twenty shots pumped into him in a matter of seconds. Snakes out here are as common as dogs in Philadelphia.

Another story I like and I saw this happen. Out here your bathroom is a hole dug in the ground with a board across it. One fellow was using the bathroom, and another fellow came in and sat besides beside him. This other fellow said, "Hey Bob that fellow is going to get that Big Horned Toad." Bob looked over and saw a big Bull Snake. Bull snakes are big but harmless. But I guess Bob did not know that. Bob jumped up, pulled up his pants, and started to run, but not far.

His pants fell down around his ankles. And Bob fell right into a bed of cactus. Bob was all covered with his own you know what, and a body full of stickers. From that day on Bob was known as crappy legs.

Another thing we did to amuse ourselves was this. We would go out hunting for Tarantula Spiders. Some of these spiders were as big as your hand. We would get a black one, a gray one put them together. And they would fight to the death. Funny thing though a black would not fight another black, nor a gray another gray.

I had been out here for fourteen months, and got a transfer. I was going up the trail a much wiser Hombre. I was going to Fort Clark, Texas.

Chapter 9
Full of half breeds

When I arrived at Fort Clark I was told I could go to the town. As soon as I took care of my horse. Well me and the others that came from Camp J.D Mann took care of our horses, and headed for town. We went to the town of Brackettville.

Brackettville was a big city. It had five saloons and was one block long. In the saloons there was gambling, poker, dice, faro, and the girls. The first saloon I went into was full of half-breeds. They were mostly Seminole Indian women up from Florida. Around Fort Clark the place was full of them. The girls started buzzing around me as soon as I walked in. Being around the soldiers most of the time they spoke pretty good English. Of course they were all good looking, and dressed mighty fine. Some had a face that would stop an eight-day clock, and their dress was an old burlap sack thrown over their shoulders.

There are a lot of stories about the girls you find in a saloon. I like this one about the soldier, and the girl with the kinky hair. Seems like the soldier was with the girl, and kept complaining about her kinky hair. Finally the girl got fed up with this and said, "What the hell do you expect for fifty cents! Seal skin?" The girls would come up to you and say, "Going to buy me a drink soldier boy? Want to have a good time soldier boy?" Well some of the boys wanted to have a good time as the place was soon half-full. The soldiers would buy lots of beer go to the girl's casa, and have a good time.

Over in the corner of the saloon was a darkie with a mouth organ in his mouth, and playing the piano at the same time. He would bang the piano, and yell like hell. At the same time the professor is banging away on the piano and shouting, the girls shouting and screaming, and the soldiers are whooping it up. Nothing like it in the world! I always have a good time in a saloon. The place we were in was called the Blue Goose.

While we were there three cowpunchers came in, and called me and a couple of soldiers over for a beer. They asked us where we came from and we said, "Sixty miles down on the Rio Grande." "Any trouble down there?" they asked. "No." We said. "Things were pretty quiet, just Indians doing some cattle rustling, and Mexicans running dope."

Just about then, in came some sheepherders. The sheepherders started shooting their mouths off about the cattlemen. And the next thing I knew, one hell of a fight broke out! In those days they had spittoons on the floor. Some of the spittoons were about three feet tall looked like a big vase. One of the fellows plunged his hand into the spittoon, and started to swinging it. One hell of a weapon as he was beating everybody!

Speaking of weapons, the cowpunchers had their weapons on. But the sheepherders did not. Out here you do not normally shoot an unarmed man. And you did not pull your weapon unless you were going to use it.

So I guess the cowpunchers did not use their guns because the sheepherders did not have theirs on. Speaking of guns reminds me of the story of the dude from the east.

This dude was in a saloon and asked the old barkeep. "Do you think I will need a gun while I am out here?" The old barkeep looked at him and said, "Well son. You may not need a gun for a week. You may not need it for a month. And you may not need it for a year. But when you need it, you need it damn quick!"

After the fight was over the place was a mess. I found out from the barkeep he had taken the guns off the sheepherders early in the day. Lucky for some he did that as there could have been a few dead bodies laying around.

Chapter 10

Four quarts of whiskey

Well we all left the Blue Goose, and walked across the street to another nice place. This place had a dirt floor. I was standing at the bar having a drink. When all of a sudden, the doors burst open, and in rode two cowboys. They rode straight up to the bar and shouted, "Give us all a drink! Me and my buddy Sol and the soldier boys!" Well the barkeep set up drinks all around. And put some beer in a bucket for the horses. The old cowpunchers started getting pretty drunk, and one shouted, "Give us all another drink, and four quarts of whiskey! Two for me and two for Sol!" They said they just got paid off after a long hard drive up the trail. All of a sudden, they wheeled their horses around fired a couple of shots in the ceiling, and out the door they rode. They rode down the street fired a few shots at the hoosegow, and rode out of town. I liked the cowpunchers they always treated me fair and square. Buy you a drink and would help you out. They were independent old boys, and generally good-natured. Just like to raise a little hell when they came off a drive. After the cowpunchers had rode off, a man came up to the bar and said, "Those damn cowpunchers! One of them horses kicked my table, and knocked over my beer!" We all turned and looked at him. Then the old barkeep pulled out his gun. Hit the cowboy over the head with the butt and said, "What the hell are you doing in here on two feet anyways!"

I was talking to one cowpuncher. And he told me the story about this arrogant old man he worked for. He said he only worked an hour for him. Here is what he told me. The old man called to him. "Hey! Come over here Bill. You are new here and I want to explain things to you. I am a man of few words. So when you hear me whistle you come running, do not stand there looking at me. When I whistle you come running to where I am." Bill said, "Why that is mighty interesting! I am a man of few words myself. Now when you whistle, and I shake my head this way you old bastard. That means I ain't coming!" Well me and the others had a good time in town. Then back to the post.

The next morning it was drill and stables, and then down to the swimming hole. The swimming hole was behind the stables about two hundred yards away. It was a pond fed by a large creek. A lot of the Indian girls from town would swim in this pond. The girls would go in the water naked. Even though they were half-breeds they were still girls, and we would watch them. One fellow got the nerve to go in the water with them. Pretty soon we were all in the water fooling about with the girls. One of the fellows ended up on the far bank with one of the girls, doing you know what. Well time went by so quick on the bank. You can imagine how it was, if you were in the water with a bunch of naked girls. It did not cost you anything either. When payday came around it was a different story.

When you went to town the girls would find you, and wanted money for your swim lessons. Live and learn. The girls did not have to look too hard for you as the whole town was only seventy-five feet long. Take away the post office and the hoosegow, and all that would be left would be the saloon.

Payday night was the best time in a saloon. So much is going on at one time, music, drinking, gambling fighting, and naturally the girls. Gambling was one thing the soldiers loved to do that and drinking. There are a lot of ways to lose your money as the soldier usually lost his.

Bucking The Tiger was a popular game. This is a card game named Faro. The cards are dealt from a box. Most boxes have a drawing of a tiger on it. So if you were playing Faro you were Bucking the Tiger. It is a simple game, but the soldier boys usually lost. They also shot dice, played Stud and Draw Poker, Blackjack and Spanish Monte.

Most games were on the up and up. But some were not. Plus you had the professional gambler. Who could clean you out pretty quick. You hear tales of big pots in poker, but I heard a tale of a pot in Montana that was unusual. One of the fellows playing wanted to call a bet, but he ran out of money. He talked the other player into accepting a personal item in lieu of money. This was accepted, but unfortunately the poor fellow lost the hand. And also his personal item, his false teeth. I guess the winner thought if I take an IOU and he loses. I will be stuck with this piece if worthless paper. If he loses he is more likely to buy back his teeth then his IOU.

On the nights the bar was bursting open at the seams. Beer was dumped into a big tub, and the glasses dipped in the tub in order to fill them quicker. The swimming instructors would be buzzing around. "Buy me a drink soldier boy! Oh soldier boy win me a new dress!" Well as you can imagine it did not take much convincing to go to their casa. Those they did not go for indoor swimming lessons usually stayed drinking and gambling. Always in the corner was some guy playing piano, yelling and shouting some kind of song. You would whip it up in town and stay as long as your money or you lasted.

The next day when you woke up you were sick as hell, sick and broke. In addition to being sick and broke, you would have to get up and go out in the hot sun. And do horse drill. But let me tell you it was all worth it.

While I was here at Fort Clark you could get a pass every night until seven the next morning. Sometimes you had to pull stable detail. This detail lasted from seven Saturday morning until seven Monday morning. During this time you would have to take care of the horses. If you had the money you could pay someone to do this duty for you. I pulled this duty many times just to earn the money. Drinking and swimming lessons can be expensive.

Woke up one morning and the sergeant told me I was being transferred. Me and others were being sent to Eagle Pass, Texas, Fort Duncan. About thirty-five miles down the Rio Grande. On the day we left for Eagle Pass all the girls from town came out to say goodbye to us. They cried, "Oh baby come back to me when you get discharged! Oh baby I will miss you hurry back." Even though the girls were half-breeds, they were ok. They did your washing for you. And many a time if you were broke they would buy a drink for you. And give you swimming lessons. I was going to miss those Brackettville girls.

Chapter 11
The evils of drink

The girls at Eagle Pass were a different bunch from the Brackettville girls. They were a pretty decent bunch and if they went swimming, they wore some clothes not like the other girls. Boys we did miss those Brackettville girls.

Our duties at Eagle Pass was to guard the border between Mexico and the States. Most of the time all we did was shoot black bears. The Mexicans were slipping over the border in small boats. They were selling dope and silk hankies. Silk and dope were very cheap. You could buy two silk hankies for a quarter. I did not bother with the dope. That stuff could mess up your head in a minute, strange stuff. We were drinking mescal that is all we needed to mess up our heads.

Mescal was made from cactus and was like drinking liquid lightning. But I liked it. In a class all by itself was whiskey sold to the Indians. To make this stuff you would take:

One barrel of water
Two gallons of raw alcohol
Two ounces of strychnine
Five bars of soap to give it bubbles
Half a pound of red peppers to give it some kick

Whiskey was called firewater by the Indians. Because a little bit of whiskey was thrown on the flame to see if it would catch fire and flame up. If it flamed up from the alcohol the Indians knew they were getting some kind of whiskey, and not flavored water. The stuff we drank (mescal and whiskey) had many different names: Red dynamite, guaranteed to blow your head off. Joy juice, a single drink would be tempted to steal his own clothes. Two would make him bite his own ears off. And three would instill a desire to save his drowning mother-in-law. Block and tackle, this would make you walk a block, and tackle anything. There was also widow maker, wolf whiskey, pine top, stump puller, gut warmer, and neck oil. Red eye, scamper juice, nose paint, tonsil varnish, tornado juice, stagger soup, Kickapoo jubilee juice, fool water, and snake bite medicine.

After taking a drink a person was said to get drunked up. Pickled or blossomed nosed or struck with bottle fever. He suffered an attack of the jim-jams. He painted his nose and rusted his boiler. Went booze blind. He was so drunk he had to open his shirt collar to piss. He slept his jag off, and woke up feeling as if a cat had kittens in his mouth. Or he breakfasted with a coyote.

Old timers used to talk about the remedies and cure alls' in the streets of some cow towns. You would find little old ladies who would curse the demon rum drinkers. But they would be tottering on their legs, and did not have all their cards in a deck. One of these remedies was Hostetters Bitters. It was sold by the drink and was suppose to cure chilblains, dyspeptic, your liver, evil humors, and loose bowels. The Hostetters Bitters was double distilled whiskey flavored with honey. Another potent medicine was Dr. Kendall's Blackberry Balsam, a remedy for cholera, biliousness, diarrhea, and dysentery. The alcohol content was sixty-one percent, and it also contained opium. Other cure alls' were also high in the alcohol content such as Ague Bitters, The Colonel's Prickly Ash Bitters, Dr. King's New Discovery for Consumption, Indian Sachems Electric Health Restorer, Indian Snake Oil, Dr. Miles Heart Cure, Mrs. Winslow's Soothing Syrup, and many others. No wonder thee little old ladies were staggering around and seemed to have lost their marbles.

Some saloons were pretty good others just dumps like the Blue Goose. A lot of saloons had false fronts, they were built to look like a two story building. But they did not have a second floor. The old saloon was known by many names, Bughouse, Jug house, Whiskey Mill, Whoop Up, Cantina, Waterhole, Pouring Spout, and a whole lot more. The name depends on where you came from.

There was a Bit House where a drink costs a quarter. Or a Short Bit House where the drink costs half a quarter. A Barrel House was a saloon where they sold whiskey straight from the barrel. A Deadfall Saloon was a place with a bad reputation. A Day and Night Saloon was a place that never closed. Enough about saloons and drinking, I did enough in my day.

I cannot remember how long I was at Eagle Pass. But one day I was told I was being transferred. I could not believe what I was told. I was going back to good old Fort Clark. Good old Brackettville and good old Brackettville girls. All the way up the trail to Fort Clark me, and the others who were transferred along with me, were talking about the girls, the town, swimming, and the saloons.

We arrived at Fort Clark and let me tell you it did not take long for us to get ready to go to town. We hit the town and had one hell of a good time. The girls were there waiting for us. As usual there was drinking and gambling, and indoor swim lessons. Some of the boys got back to camp at midnight, others got back at seven in the morning. And again this depended on how long your money could hold out.

The next day at roll call the First Sergeant said, "Get ready to leave at nine this morning for Fort Apache, Arizona." It felt like we got hit with a twelve-inch gun. It came as a complete surprise to us. They did not even let us go back into town to say good-bye to the girls. The girls came out to say good-bye to us. They wished us well and whooped us out of town.

Chapter 12

Fort Apache

I arrived at Fort Apache. And what a hell of a place nothing but soldiers and Indians. Plenty of Indians twenty-three thousand at Fort Apache, and one-hundred miles east of us was another reservation. That had eighteen-thousand Indians on it. Most of the buildings were old Dolby buildings, better known as the Dolby Shacks. They are simple made out of mud and grass. The bathrooms were a block or so from the barracks.

After you went to the bathroom it fell into a box below. And every morning some Indian came around with a cart, and emptied the boxes into a cart. I said to one of the fellows, "I think the Indians are putting this crap on their vegetables. What do you think of that?" He said, "I usually put salt, pepper, and butter on mine." We had a good laugh over his remark.

We were about ninety- five miles from the town of Holbrook. Holbrook had a railroad, a post office, general merchandise store, saloons, freight office, and naturally a Hoosegow. Just about all towns had a Hoosegow. Most soldiers called them City Hall. About ten miles from Ft. Apache was a place called Pine Top. And that is all there was out there, pine trees.

On the fort was a sawmill. Every three weeks a detail was sent out to cut down some trees. A team of Mule Skinners would haul the trees off Pinetop, until we cut down the number of trees required. Let me tell you this was no easy job. Other fellows at the sawmill cut the trees into lumber. Most fellows including me did not know a damn thing about working a sawmill. You learned awful quick how to cut lumber, or cut your fingers, or hand off. I did not have any accidents at the sawmill. But others did.

Luckily I was sent to Pine Top only twice in the time I was at Fort Apache. Also maybe once or twice in three years you got to guard the Paymasters Wagon. Usually there was a total of thirty men guarding the Pay Wagon. Twenty

Cavalry and ten Infantry. I was certainly glad I was in the Cavalry, and could ride my horse during this guard duty. The Infantrymen had to sit in the wagon with a board across it for a seat. Going down the trail it would shake your guts out. The roads were nothing but mud tracks up the valley, and down the ravines. Rough as hell! We went to meet the Denver train stopping at Holbrook. The wagon was pulled by six mules driven by a Muleskinner.

The skinner had a big whip and would crack the lead mule over the ears. He would not hit the mule's ear but came close to it. I think the mules would have run all day for the Muleskinner. We made three stops on the way, and then into the town of Holbrook. You could have a good time in Holbrook if you had the money. We all used to borrow money when you had this detail. There were people in camp who would lend you five dollars and you had to pay them back six dollars. It was a steep rate of interest, but it was worth it. We met the 7:10 train from Denver. We would drive the wagon right up on the platform. The ten Infantry men would line up with loaded rifles and pistols, five on each side while the money was being loaded. After the money was loaded the Infantrymen would ride in the wagon. And the Cavalry is stationed to the front, rear, and both sides of the wagon. We were carrying about one hundred thousand in twenty dollar gold pieces. The gold pieces were transported inside of canvas bags.

Most of the time we tried to ride our horses at a trot. The men who were picked for this duty had to have at least two years military service. Most of the fellows I went with on this trip had between fifteen and twenty year's service. We were traveling through open country and we knew there was a danger of robbery. But to my way of thinking it would be a damn hard job to rob us. Here we were thirty soldiers all armed. I never heard of a robber's gang having more than five members. I am quite sure we could have beaten the robbers at their own game if we were to get robbed. You can bet your bottom dollar the word of the robbery would quickly spread. And the soldiers would soon be on the trail of the robbers. In addition to paying the troops we also paid the Indians for the work they did at the fort.

Chapter 13

The Banker and the Indian

When we sit around shooting the breeze there are a lot of stories told. I like this story about an Indian and a Banker. Seems like this Indian, went into a bank to borrow some money. The Banker told him, "You have to have some valuable property before we lend you any money?" The Indian asked, "What kind of property?" The Banker said, "Land is valuable and so are horses and cattle." The Indian replied, "I got plenty horses!" The Banker said, "How many?" "Over five- hundred." replied the Indian. "Well we can lend you the money on your horses. And the bank will own the horses if you do not pay us back the money you borrowed."

Well the Indian borrowed the money, and put up his horses. Later on he came into the bank, to pay back the money he borrowed. He paid the bank and his horses were returned to him. The Banker noticed the Indian had some money left over. The Banker asked, "What are you going to do with the money you have left over?" "Keep it." replied the Indian. The Banker went on to explain about putting the money in the bank and earning interest. The Indian agreed to this. Just before he handed over the money to the Banker he grabbed him by the arm and said, "Where are your horses for me?"

Chapter 14

Died from want of water

Things are tough out here. Out here you climb for water and dig for wood. The wood is all brushwood. And only the root will burn. The water is rainwater that comes down from the mountains and collects in rock pools. Water springs are far and few between. You will go many a mile before you come across water nothing but sagebrush, sand, and stone. Some of the sand flats are twenty miles long and sixty miles wide.

Out in this country you have to look out for your horse. Making sure he does not go down and out on you for the lack of water. If your horse goes down you are in big trouble. Big trouble is when you are only ten miles from camp, and your horse goes down. And you only have one canteen of water. Now if you walk the ten miles in the desert sun you are a goner for sure. You do not have any water left. And you do not know where to get any. Pretty soon your tongue starts to swell up. Your eyes start to sting, and you end up walking in circles. Next thing you go buggy you start seeing things that are not there. You see in the desert flats everything looks the same. And the more you look around the worse it gets. You become confused. You keep pushing your swollen tongue up in your mouth. Your eyes stinging seeing things that are not there, and then you go down for the count. I know because all this happened to me. Luckily I made it back to camp. Usually what happens if you die in the desert someone will find you, a soldier, a cowpuncher, or an Indian. Cause of death is listed as "Died from want of water". There is an old saying out here. Keep your head and give your horse his head. These horses were born and raised out here. I will tell you a tale later about the time I did not give my horse his head.

Sometimes the whole troop would be sent out on the desert along with pack train of mules. These mules carry all our gear for cooking and eating plus hay and oats for the horses. We take about twenty troops and some men who are called Packers. These Packers are hard to find and when you have them you want to keep them. They are experts on loading a Pack Mule. They use a certain kind of grass for padding the mules' sides with, in order not to injure the mule. They load about two- hundred and fifty pounds "or so" pounds on each mule. And put a little halter on the mule. Usually the mule is blindfolded prior to loading him up. After a mule is loaded the mule is turned loose, and they just stand around waiting for the others to get loaded. After all their mules are loaded the Head Packer tells the Captain of the Troops, and off we go.

The pack train follows behind us. With the Pack Train Chief, and his bell mare in the lead. They always have a mare with a bell around its neck. The pack train mules always follow the sound of the bell. We only use pack trains when we cannot use wagons.

Now these little old Pack Mules are pretty damn smart when they are going along a mountain trail. They are awful careful not to bump into anything because if they do, they may fall off the side of the mountain. We have often gone into the mountains with a Prairie Schooner pulled by six mules. Now let me tell you it is no easy job driving a Prairie Schooner around a mountainside. There is only one rein, and it is attached to the left front mule. Many a time we had to put a rope on the wagon with twenty men pulling on the rope. Just to make sure the wagon did not tip over on its side. Getting back to the Pack Mule, he steps very carefully. He will stop and wiggle his foot, and feel his way along. These mules could make twelve to fifteen miles a day in the mountains.

Chapter 15

Do not let the eye go down

One day a courier came into Fort Apache. With the message that some white men had killed an Indian Chief at Cibicue Creek. The Indians at Cibicue Creek are a duff bunch. They were a bunch of thieves who would steal anything they could get their hands on.

Cibicue is about thirty miles from Apache and twenty- two or so miles from the town of Globe. Me and about fifteen others plus some Indian Scouts were led by Lt. Fenton to go to Cibicue Creek.

We got there about sundown and things looked pretty bad for us. The Indians were crying, hollering, and dancing in front of a blazing fire. Boy things were getting hot. An old Scout came over, and told us to keep our hands away from our pistols. As the Indians were very mad at all white men, and could go on the warpath at anytime. All at once, twenty or thirty young Indian bucks came out on their ponies waving their rifles. The U.S. Government gave the Indians the rifles to hunt with. We sat looking at the Indians, and they were looking at us. There was seven hundred of them and twenty or so of us. Well, I guess you know how I felt. Two years in the military, and it is all going to end here! These Indians are mean, most time they do not come to Apache, and get their rations. One of our Indian Scouts told us we had better get down over the hill by the creek.

The scouts name was Skippy Joe. We had another scout with us by the name of Peaches. Peaches was an aide to the famous Indian Geronimo, but Peaches was also one of the scouts who helped track Geronimo down. After he left the reservation in the early 1880's, and was playing holy hell in the territories.

We went over the hill and Lt. Fenton told us, "Don't let your eyes go down!" That meant do not go to sleep. And keep our horses saddled, and our weapons loaded. He figured we might be attacked at any time. I guess you know it was a long night for us.

The Indians had their fire blazing all night and were dancing around the fire. The old chief was lying in front of the fire. Boys the hours seemed like days. We could not sleep even if told we could. In the morning we were so dam scared as we did not know what was going to happen.

At daybreak Lt. Fenton said, "Come on boys let's get out of here!" Let me tell you it did not take long to get out of there. So off we went to Globe to arrest two men. Bill Voris, and Hank Ketchersides. On the trail we saw some cowmen and told them what was happening. We had an all day ride ahead of us. Soon in a short while we stopped and had breakfast fed and watered the horses. After breakfast we began to feel a little better. We saddled up and off to Globe we went.

We made Globe before sundown and rode up to the shack where Frank and Bill were. One man came out. Lt. Fenton said, "Are you Bill Voris, and Hank Ketchersides?" The man replied, "I am Bill, Frank is inside. Have you come to arrest us?" "Yes." Lt. Fenton said. "Well we will be ready in half an hour. Just want to fix a few things up for the boys when they come in. Want to tell them what to do?" Bill and Frank were soon ready to go and Frank asked, "Where do you want us to ride?" "Ride wherever you want to and you can ride with any soldier you want to." said Lt Fenton. Luckily, Bill rode next to me and told me about the killing. Here is his story. I cannot remember all of it. But it is pretty close to what he said.

Bill said he was the one who killed the Indian Chief. He and Frank went to Cibicue Creek to talk to the chief about some trouble they had been having with things being stolen. As they rode into the Indian camp they were met by a bunch of young bucks. Bill told the young bucks he wanted to speak to the chief. Both Frank and Bill were sitting on their horses. The chief came over and all of a sudden, the chief made a grab for Bill's rifle. One of the young bucks fired a shot over Bill's head. And Bill pulled his pistol and shot the chief who dropped to the ground. He and Frank rode out of the camp very fast. Bill said he never rode his horse so fast and hard. Bill figured the darkness saved their lives.

Off we headed for Globe. All of a sudden Bill shouted, "Lt. Fenton you are heading the wrong way for us boys. We cannot go past their camp. As it will be a murder for me and Frank, and probably some of your soldiers." Bill and Frank were right. If we went back the way the Lt. started out, we would go right by Cibicue.

Something in our pants began to feel soft while we waited to see what the Lt. was going to do. Go back up the trail past the Indians camp? Or go by Globe and San Carlos. The Globe and San Carlos route was about a one- hundred and sixty mile trip, about sixty miles to San Carlos, and one- hundred over the summit to Fort Apache. Well Bill, Frank, and the Lt. talked it over and thought it best to take the long trip back to Fort Apache. It took us almost a week to get back to the fort.

We turned in Bill and Frank over to the commander. We were finished with that trip and we all went go have a nice bath. We told Skippy Joe, Peaches, and another Scout we had with us named Chicken Hawk we would take them on a hunting trip to Rucker's Canyon.

A couple of days later the parade ground was full of squatting Indians. They were waiting to see Bill and Frank get shot, Bill and Frank were not on the post. They were turned loose the day before and were probably back in Globe. We told the Indians that Frank and Bill were in jail and would never get out. The Indians started jabbering. And then all of a sudden, up they got and went out of camp.

Chapter 16

The great stampede

One time I was detailed to be head guard of the animals. This is a detail where you take all the horses and mules out of camp and let them graze. Well there was me and three others doing this duty. We turned the horses and mules out of the camp. And they ran like hell towards the flats about two miles away.

Off to our left was a canyon it was about 60 feet wide, and thirty feet deep. As headman I was told to watch out for the canyon, and not to let the horses fall in to it. I thought this is an easy detail. All of a sudden, the mules started kicking, and running. Then the horses started to run all of them heading straight for the canyon. You see a mule farts while he is grazing. And when he farts he kicks his back legs up. Soon they start running which in turn gets the horses running, and you have a stampede. We worked like hell trying to stop the stampede. I thought they are all going to end up at the bottom of the canyon. And I will be in big trouble when I got back, if I went back.

I was riding for all I was worth. When the next thing I knew I was looking into the eyes of an old Indian, and his squaw. Who were trying to give me some water. My horse hit a soft spot, and I went flying off at full speed. I was ok just got the wind knocked out of me. I looked around and there were the horses, and mules grazing again as if nothing happened. One of the other fellows on this duty told me the animals just stopped on their own. They did not see what happened to me as they were too busy chasing the horses and mules. All of a sudden, up they jumped again. But this time they were heading for the fort at a full gallop. I thought this is all I need. I could picture the animals going through the fort at a full gallop wrecking things. Well these old devils knew the ropes. And they just slowed down, and put themselves in the corral and stables as if nothing happened.

Shortly after my time with the stampede, me and a man named George took a three-month leave and went out to Pine Top. George and me planned to do some hunting and fishing. We took a week to build a cabin. This was a damn good cabin not some lean type of affair plenty of timber plenty of honey. We hunted for squirrels, wild turkeys, pheasants, deer, and bear. You could fish for all the Mountain Trout you could want.

George and me did this for three months. Everything was fine until one day a young Indian boy walked into our cabin. He had something wrong with his arm, crooked like. His camp was a little way up the canyon from out cabin. He was looking around the cabin, and then picked up George's hunting knife as if to look at it. The boy started to leave and George shouted, "Where is my knife!" The boy made out he did not know what George was talking about. So George socked him really hard. The boy yelled and ran out of the cabin.

An old prospector nearby told us George had hit the Chief's son. That was enough for me and George. We told the prospector to take care of our stuff, and send it in with the next logging party. George and me made tracks back to the post. We told our Captain what happened. And he said the Indians would have parted out hair down the middle if they caught us.

One day me and some other fellows were riding along between the east and north forks of the White River. We saw a hole in the side of the mountain about five hundred feet We all thought it was a bear hole and we were a little scared to go in.

Well we climbed up and went in. We did not see any traces of a bear. We took a lantern and some rope in with us. The fellow in the lead with the lantern said, "It's just like a little alley in here." Then we saw a room about eight feet by eight feet and seven feet high. The room looked like water had washed it out from time to time.

In this room was a little mound that looked like a beehive. In the beehive was a lot of little bones, skulls, legs, and arms. Scattered around was a lot of broken pottery with all colors of paint on them. They looked like jugs you would carry water in. Also there were a lot of arrowheads scattered around. We saw eight or ten more of these rooms and they all looked alike. They went back a long way in the mountain.

They must have been awful small people. No one seemed to know anything about them. They were not cliff dwellers. Boys it would scare you to go through the place we called the alley. We took some of the skulls, and used them as a tobacco box. The skulls were about as big as a grapefruit.

I wish I could write down all the funny things I saw out here. The things nature made from sand, stone, and water. You see I do not know how to spell the names of these things and do not know how to word it. If I could, I could write a pretty nice story about Texas, Arizona, New Mexico, and Utah.

Chapter 17

Jess, you're a good horseman

An interesting trip I had was to the Black Mountains in Arizona, by way of New Mexico, and Utah. The Black Mountains are up by Lake Mead in Arizona running along the Colorado River. I was at Fort Wingate at this time. Fort Wingate is in the New Mexico Territory. We left Fort Wingate heading for Gallup, New Mexico. At Gallup we were joined by a regiment From Fort Apache, and some troops from the San Carlos Indian Reservation. We had about fourteen- hundred men lots of wagons, and a mule train. We were going into the Black Mountains to take the Indians who left the reservation, back to their reservation.

There are a lot of antelope out here and one day my sergeant said to me, "Jess you're a good horseman see those antelope out there? I want you and another fellow to go round them up. And bring them in here, so we can have some fresh meat to eat." I never heard of rounding up antelope. But I figured the sergeant must know what he is talking about. So me and this other fellow named Jim went off to round them up.

They were about a half a mile out. But it seemed like Jim and me never got any closer to them than a half-mile away. Finally I told Jim to circle around one way. I would circle around the other way and we could close in on them. When I gave the word we both galloped after them to round them up. Do not let anyone tell you that you can round up antelope. Jim and me chased them sons of bitches all over that day. Damn near killed my horse got thrown off five times, and had one heck of a long ride back to camp. When we got back we both got ribbed, seems like they pull this trick on anyone dumb enough to fall for it.

Out on the desert it is hot, and water is scarce. We came across a water-hole. But the Captain would not let us drink from them. He said, "If there is not enough water for all of us there is not enough water for one of us." The Captain would stand over the water hole with his pistol drawn to make sure no one got any water. Out here you could shoot a man for a drink of water. We had some very long drives. The biggest jump we made was thirty-one miles in one day. Let me tell you something that is doing some traveling to cover thirty-one miles with wagons. U.S. Cavalry boys could cover forty miles a day if we had to, but not with wagons. On the wagons they had big water barrels that we would fill up for the mules, but us Cavalry boys and their horses had to wait until we hit a river. We had Indian Scouts with us who knew the territory, but you still had a long ride to get water.

We traveled as far as we could with the wagons, and then we switched to pack mules. The country was pretty rough. And a wagon train just could not get up into the mountains. Pretty soon the pack mules could not get up into the mountains either. So we rode our horses. The trail was narrow and steep. It was like riding through little alleys you find behind houses in Philadelphia. Not much water or grass for the horses either.

Chapter 18
These two Chinks

The only cooking tools we took with us was a frying pan, and a coffee pot. We had feed for the horses one cup of grain a day. We had to feed our horses what we called bunch grass. Little bunches of grass here and there. It would take a man weeks to gather a basketful. The only thing we could cook was flat cakes. Flat cakes are made with flour, grease, salt, and baking powder. It was tough eating, but you could eat at least three of these flat cakes. The poor horses nearly starved. These poor horses got so thin that you had to fold your blanket under your horse, in order to cinch up your saddle.

We passed a few places where prospectors had been panning for gold. We rode a long way on the trail, and finally came to a wide-open area. It was about three or four miles wide. We were now in the foothills of the Black Mountains. There were a lot of sand dunes. They looked like big rollers (waves) that you would see on the beach at Atlantic City in New Jersey. They were very pretty, and when the sun shined on them they would change colors. Soon we came to a little alley again only this time it was different. Imagine you are looking up the side of a mountain about three- hundred feet high. You look for a place to go through, but you do not see any. All of a sudden, there is a little alley for you to ride through.

The Indian Scouts told us the good man (god) made the alleys for big chiefs to ride through. This little trail would twist and turn, and many times came out to the edge of the mountain. I would look down and think! What the hell am I doing here? In places it was like going through a tunnel, and then it would open up and twist around again.

We saw a lot of mountain goats up here, but no Indians. The scouts said this was the place where all Indians hid from the government. The Indians hiding could see us a day before we got to where they were. The mountain goats belonged to the Indians who would sell the goat hides. I thought to myself, who the hell are they selling them to?

I soon found out! At the bottom of a hill we saw a little shack. And in this shack were two Chinamen who ran the general store. They sold calico goods, flour, tea, sugar, tobacco, cotton, pipes, needles, and lord knows what else. They probably sold whiskey too, but we did not see any. These two Chinks spoke the Indian language, and traded with the Indians. The Indians did not know the value of money. And traded deer, bobcat, wolf, and mountain lion hides, for what the Chinamen sold in their store. Some other Chinamen would come in with pack burros to take goods in and out. Where they came from, I have no idea. We fed and watered our horses at the Chinamen's post, and headed out again going higher into the mountains.

Soon we came across a log cabin and best of all a fine water spring. We camped for the night by the cabin. Breakfast in the morning was flat cakes, and coffee, bunch grass for the horses. The Captain said, "If you got hungry enough you could eat bunch grass." I thought what the hell do people use for brains. There was not enough bunch grass for horses, let alone a man. We stayed at the cabin another day. Me and some other fellows carved our names on a rock near the cabin. Finally we came across some Indians, but not the Indians we were looking for. This is where we got our red stones, they are called garnets. The Indians have lots of these stones, and would trade them for some Bull Durham tobacco and cigarette papers. The Indians said they got the garnets from ant-hills. Up here they have big red ants. The ants in building their nests would bring the stones up, and throw them outside the nest. And the Indians would gather them up.

We left the Indians and came across some big white sand. Nearby was also some water. We had a little fun on these sand hills. We would run and belly flop on the sand just like belly flopping on the snow. For supper we had the same old thing, flat cakes and coffee. We would give the meals hell when we got back to the post. I forgot to mention there was only twenty of us Cavalry boys that went into the mountains. The captain said we were the first white troops to ever set foot in the Black Mountains. Where the Indians were hiding was anybody's guess. As far as I knew they did not do any harm to anyone. The only thing they would harm would be another Indian.

I slept at night on the sand hills. See nothing, hear nothing, do nothing, and eat nothing. One day we pulled out for the main camp. Same kind of country on the way out and the way in. When we arrived back in the camp everyone was asking us what it was like up there. We said the factory is shut down. And everyone went home, nothing there. We ate good that night. Next day off to the pack train camp then to the wagon train camp, and then back to Gallup. I went back to Fort Wingate. The others back to Fort Apache and the San Carlos. Soon after that trip, I was sent to Fort Huachuca, Arizona.

Chapter 19
Burn the calf between the toes

One day I was detailed to go to Slaughter's Ranch. Old man Slaughter had a sixty- five thousand acre ranch, part of it in Mexico, and part of it in Arizona. Frank Slaughter was a retired lawman. He called on the government as he was having some trouble with people rustling his cattle. Mr. Slaughter thought it was some of the fellows he sent to jail while he was Sheriff trying to get even with him. If I remember correctly old man Slaughter adopted a young Indian lad. And the boy grew up, and ended up killing Mr. Slaughter.

Well there was me, six other Cavalry boys, three Indian Scouts on the way to old man Slaughters ranch. I got to thinking about cattle rustlers. There is a saying out here. All a man needs to start a herd is a running iron, a rope, a horse, and the nerve to use them. Rustling cattle was not just a matter of round- ing up the cattle. The rustler had ways of making rustling an art.

One was to open up a bunch of calves, and drive their mothers away. They would also slit the tongue of the calf, so it could not suck. Or would cut the eyelid muscles, so they could not see their mothers. They would also burn the calf between the toes, so they could not follow their mother. The calf, whose tongue was slit, would soon learn to eat grass. You could tell the calf that had its eyelid muscle slit as the muscle would heal up, but the calf had droopy eye. In either case the main idea was to separate the calf from its mother. And then the rustler would place his brand on the calf.

The rustler had to be good at changing brands. To do this they used an iron bar called a running iron. This was an iron bar with a curved end. Or they would also use a piece of telegraph wire, and also cinch rings. They could also use a temporary brand by cutting away the hair with a knife. Many times they would cold brand a calf. To cold brand a calf they would use the owners' real branding iron. Many rustlers worked for a man, but would later steal his cattle. They would cold brand cattle by using a wet blanket, and the branding iron.

The wet blanket stopped the brand from being burned into the hide, but would singe the hair. It looked like a good brand, good enough to fool the owner. After the hair grew back in the rustler would brand the cattle with his own brand.

The rustler had a few names. Such as Brand Burner, Brand Blotter, Brand Artist. And he was said to swing a wide loop. The rustler had to do a good job on his branding as he had to fool some expert cowmen. A botched brand could be very unhealthy.

When the rustler was working over a brand and a rider approached in the distance. The rider was waved around by the rustler. He did this by waving his hat in a semi-circle from left to right. This meant keep on riding stranger unless you want trouble. If the rustler got caught he usually ended up in prison, but he could also end up dead.

I started telling you we were going to Slaughter's to see about some cattle rustling, and horse stealing. Now horse stealing is an all together different thing. It did not take much hard work to steal a horse. You just stole the horse. However there is a big difference if you get caught stealing a horse, you get hanged or shot. No questions asked no if and or buts.

There is a story about some men who killed a horse thief. One fellow went out of a saloon, and could not see his horse. He thought old so and so stole my horse. He went back in the saloon, and him and his friends rode out to so and so's ranch. Even though the man did not see his horse, they ended stringing so and so up. When they returned to the saloon, one of the fellows went out the back door of the saloon. And there was the other fellow's horse that they thought was stolen. The men rode out to so and so's ranch and told his widow. "This morning we hanged your man Bob for stealing a horse. But we later found out he didn't do it. I guess the joke is on us."

Chapter 20

Him catch big one, Him catch big one

We looked all through the hills and what have you looking for signs of a white man. You can tell from the way a campfire is made who made it, an Indian or a white man. It is very hard to tell at times. But our Indian Scouts could tell.

Speaking of the Indians let me tell you this. We had two camps of Indian Scouts, and Indian Police. The Indians did not wear pants most of the time just a little g-string. Their camps were about a block apart facing one another, both about three blocks from our barracks.

We got paid every two months, soldiers and Indians. Every payday the Indians would get drunk on what we called Doodle Pre. Doodle Pre was Indian beer, twice as strong as beer. Smelled like rum, and tasted like hell. Well the Indians would get drunk, and start shooting one another.

Now let me tell you it is not a lot of fun to go down to where the drunken Indians are and take their weapons away from them. After you take their weapon away you throw them in the Hoosegow for the night. They also throw the soldier boy in the Hoosegow when he gets drunk, and causes trouble. Not all the time, but sometimes. You ought to see and Indian when he is drunk. Hairy, dirty, smelly, one hell of a mess, but I liked the Indians.

When you are out on the plains like we were, we would use a thing called a heliograph to keep in contact. This is a way of talking over long distances with mirrors. We could not find anything at Slaughter's Ranch so we headed back to camp. On the way we got word by the heliograph to go to Rucker's Canyon, and flush out some bank robbers.

Rucker's Canyon was about forty miles from Slaughter's place. On the way to the canyon we stopped. At a place called Moonshine Ranch, and loaded up on mescal. We also let the Indians get some mescal. We did not drink the mescal until we made camp for the night. We sent the Indians out for some meat and soon they came back with a big buck deer. We had deer steaks, and the Indians roasted the ribs. What we could not eat we buried. Along with our steaks we had coffee, and baking soda biscuits.

The Indians were camped a little way down from us. Pretty soon we were all drinking mescal, U.S. Cavalry boys, and our Indian Scouts. We were whooping it up and having a good time. Our camp tailor Bill got up said, "I'm going to take a dump." and walked a little ways off. We were half-dippy from drinking the mescal laughing, and joking. When one of the Indian Scouts came to us drunk as hell and said, "Him catch big one, him catch a big one." We was too drunk to know what the hell he was talking about. All of a sudden, one of the fellows spotted what the Indian was ranting about. Up where old Bill was taking a dump. Was a little foothill, and on top of the foothill was a big mountain lion. Crouched down, looking at Bill. "Bill!" "Bill!" We shouted. "Look over your shoulder behind you!" Old Bill stuck his hand to his nose and waved his fingers at us.

The Indian Scout had his rifle with him and started walking towards Bill. Bill looked up and saw the mountain lion. Boys did Bill jump up quick, and try to pull his pants up, and run at the same time. The Indian Scout was too drunk to get a bead on the lion. The lion just crouched there looking at Bill and the Indian. We jumped up and the lion let out a growl. Turned and ran away.

Just think! There you are having a dump. You turn around and there is a mountain lion waiting to pounce on you. Well we all had a big laugh! About Bill and the mountain lion, and went back to drinking the mescal. The wolves were not the only things howling that night! We were all dippy, the Indians were all dippy, one hell of a night!

Chapter 21
I forgot my pistol

Up the next morning but not feeling too good off we went. On the way to the canyon we ran into some cowpunchers. Decided to stop and sat around chewing the fat. One of the cowpunchers said, "Boys about two miles out is a herd of antelope. You have good fast horses. How about going out and rounding some up? So we can have some meat." I said, "What the hell do you think we are? A bunch of greenhorns to go out and round up antelope? Besides, I tried doing that up in the Black Mountains." We all looked at one another and burst out laughing.

The Indian Scouts were out on the plains killing birds with a club something like a boomerang. The Indians built a fire out of chips, and threw the birds on the fire feathers guts and all. After they are cooked they pull the skin off. Then guts fall out, and then the Indians eat them. Damn birds are so small it takes a hundred just to get a mouthful. I did not eat any of these birds. But some of the other fellows did.

Next morning we pulled out for the canyon. We scouted the area and could not find anything. So we headed back to Slaughter's Ranch. We looked around again for the people bothering old man Slaughter, but could not find any signs of them. We stayed around the area for five days and then headed back to Fort Huachuca.

We started out feeling good as we were hitting the mescal. Most of us had a full canteen of it. Well we got about ten miles away from the ranch, when I noticed I did not have my pistol. This happens quite a bit. A big pistol, pistol belt with twenty-five rounds of ammunition. And rifle ammunition is heavy. It gets so heavy at times you just take it off, and put it on the ground near you. I told the boys to cover for me as I was going back to get my pistol.

I traveled about six or seven miles towards the ranch. And saw one of our Indian Scouts coming down the trail. The Scout had my pistol and pistol belt, and gave them to me. The Scout said, "You take water." Offering me a canteen of water, he knew I had a canteen full of mescal. "You take water maybe die." He said. So I took the water from him, and told him to go on as I wanted to rest my horse awhile.

Chapter 22

My horse wanted left, I wanted right

I rested a few hours and headed up the trail. I had a few hits of the mescal, and was feeling pretty good. About three or four miles down the trail, the trail splits. One trail to the right the other to the left. One trail would be a horse trail, and the other a cattle trail. I was too drunk to know which was which. If you took the cattle trail you would be in big trouble water became a problem. If I took the horse trail I would be ok for water. My horse wanted to go left I wanted to go right. So we went right.

It started to get dark. No place in sight, and no water for me or for my horse, nothing. My horse started to snort and whinny up, so I knew something was up. Soon I spotted and old abandoned adobe hut. The hut was half standing with a small corral, and two hitching posts. But best of all a small stream enough water for me, and the horse. I gave my horse a good drink took off his saddle, and hitched him to the post outside the hut. I gave him half of the grain I carried and saved the other half for his breakfast. You see we usually carried at least one meal of grain for the horse. Good thing I carried it this time. It was dark by now and I thought to myself. The last thing I need is for my horse to go wondering off in the night. I tied my lariat to him and the post. If my horse got away, I would be sunk.

This adobe hut was used for cutting, and branding cattle. I went inside the hut to sleep using my saddle as a pillow. I lay down and tried to get some sleep. I kept thinking about the mountain lion and Bill. So I loaded my pistol and carbine, and settled down for the night. My horse outside was pawing the ground and snorting, so I knew something was up. It was dark as hell and could not see a thing. But I kept hearing noises. I had another shot of mescal and began to think. Here I am all alone on the wrong trail and lost. I will be ok if my horse does not get away. I kept hearing these funny noises. But I could not make out what the noises were. Again I started thinking about old Bill and the mountain lion. Plus wolves, bobcats, snake, and just about everything else I had seen in this part of the country.

I stayed awake all night with my pistol at the ready. As I kept hearing these noises, and still did not know what they were. Finally daybreak! As it got lighter I could make out movement, and where it was coming from. In the fireplace across the room from me. But I could not make out what was causing the noises. Finally it got light enough for me to see what was happening. In the fireplace was three or four buzzards, flapping, and jumping about. They were chewing on an old dried cow carcass. I was glad that was all it was.

I went out fed my horse what was left of the grain, and started down the trail again. I did not have any breakfast, and I did not have any supper the night before. I was hungry, hung-over, and tired. Hell of a way to start your day! I rode for about fifteen miles stopped and gave my horse a little rest. We were lucky as on the way down we came across a water hole. So we both had a good drink. After we rested awhile, we started off again.

My horse started to whinny and snorting, so I knew something was up again. I looked around but could not see anything. We rode a long time when the horse started carrying on again. I looked around and this time, I saw a log cabin sitting by a river.

I rode up to the cabin and saw some cowpunchers. They shouted, "Hello soldier where the hell did you come from?" "Damned if I know" says I. "Left Slaughter's Ranch spent the night in an old abode hut. And here I am." They asked me if my horse needed feeding. I said, "No! But I do!" Well they took care of my horse, and fed me real good. I stayed the night with them. And the next morning I headed out again.

The foreman took me down to the river, and showed me where to cross. He asked, "How does your horse take to water?" "Good!" I said. "How does your horse do in sand?" "Good!" I said. "Alright follow me." He said. "This is where your horse can cross. Keep his head downstream. And be careful it's a little soft on the other side." I thought this is going to be fun. I had me, the saddle, and rifle, pistol belt, and ammunition, blanket, rain slicker, and my mess gear. The river was about twenty feet wide and four feet deep.

I told the foreman thanks, and waded out into the river. My horse had a hard time keeping his head above water. But finally we made it to the other side. We had a hard time getting up the bank, but my good old horse finally got to the top.

The foreman shouted over to me," Head for Nigger Mountain bear to your right. And look for the gap it will take you into Bisbee." I guess I rode about twenty miles that day with the sun beating down on me, it was no joy ride. I finally came across a water hole. I stopped to water and rest my horse. And I took his saddle off, and let him roll in the dust. Horses love doing this. I drank the last of my mescal. Rubbed my horse down saddled up, and headed out again.

I had not gone too far when my horse started acting up again. The sun was beating down but my old horse acted as if nothing happened to us. He started running like the wind. Soon we saw some other horses then some people. And the next thing I knew I was in Bisbee, Arizona. I put my horse up in the government stables where the U.S. Mail horses were kept. Fed and watered my horse, and went off to the saloon.

I had some drinks with the mail carriers. Went to supper, back to the saloon for some more drinking, and then off to bed. I stayed in the bunkhouse with the mail carriers. And bright and early the next morning I headed for Fort Huachuca.

I rode into the Fort and thought I will catch hell now. I found out I was only a day behind the others who covered for me. So I did not get into any trouble. I was so happy to be back.

Chapter 23
Captain Dodd's Monkey Drill

A fellow out here by the name of Captain Dodd invented what we called "Monkey Drill" Now this is what it is like. On the horse is a bridle. With a surcingle holding on a blanket, and that is it. You fall in by your horse and the command is given, and off you go to the bullring.

The bullring is egg shaped about two blocks long and a block wide. The man in the lead sets the pace and the others are behind in a single file. The command of trot is given. Then gallop. Then dismount, and mount. Your horses are at a gallop, and you have to mount, and dismount.

Here is how it is done. You get a lock mane in your left hand. Put your right hand on the horses' withers. At the command dismount, you throw your left leg over the horse's crop, and jump off. Hitting the ground with both feet at once, and then bounce right back up on the horses back. Again still at a gallop. Then the command of dismount vault, and mount is given. You just do the same thing as before. Except when you bounce up, you vault over the horses back. Touch the ground with both feet, and then jump up on the horses back. Then there is another command. Face to the rear, dismount, and mount. This is the time when you see a lot of people take a tumble. Most of them fall off before the about face command is given.

Let me tell you, it is a damn hard thing to do. Riding a horse backwards, and it is hard to make an about face. It is fairly easy riding around the ring at a gallop. And when you dismount, and your feet hit the ground, you soon bounce back up on the horse. As long as you have a good hold on the horses' mane, the old horse, just about pulls you back up on his back. The faster a horse gallops, the easier it is for you to bounce back up.

Soon we were jumping over two foot hurdles. Then five foot hurdles, then ditches about seven feet wide. This jumping is all done bareback. Then you do the same jumps, with a saddle on the horse. After a bit of Monkey Drill we have rescue and pick-up drill. For pick-up and pistol drill, we used old pistols. You go around the Bull Ring the same as before, but with a saddle on your horse. You start off at a walk, then trot, then gallop. The first time around you drop your pistol to the ground. When you come back around the second time, you are supposed to pick up your pistol, while your horse is at a gallop.

Now here is how it is done. You grab a lock of mane in your left hand. Put your right leg and heel around the cantle of the saddle. The cantle is the back of the saddle. You hold on with your heel. Lean all the way down almost to the ground, and grab your pistol. Mind you have to be fast to do this. Then we have rescue drill. One man stands in the middle of the ring, and is supposed to be hurt, and can help himself a little. At the same time you pretend the Indians are coming after you, and you cannot stop to tie this man to your horse. You stop your horse where the man is. Bend down with your right arm. Place all your weight on the off stirrup, and with his help, and your pulling. You get him up on your horse behind you, and off you go.

I am telling you, if you saw a bunch of Indians coming after you. Hurt or not you would soon get up on the horse. After pistol and rescue drill, we have pistol practice. We had a steel frame made to look like a man riding his horse. This frame was life size. The frame is covered with black target paper. You also have frames of a man standing, kneeling, and lying down. The first time you shoot at the target you are five yards away, then ten, fifteen, twenty, and finally twenty-five yards from the target. This is done with all the different targets. You get five points if you hit the man above the waist. Three points if you hit below the waist. You get five points anytime you hit the target of a man lying down, as only his head and shoulders are visible. I never had a problem with pistol practice. I usually got top scores.

Chapter 24

War declared on the beavers

My next assignment was to Fort Du Chesnee, Utah. Not much to do in Utah. Except the time we declared war on the beavers. There are a lot of beavers out here and let me tell you they are hard workers. We diverted water from the Du Chesnee River to make a reservoir on the post. We dug a ditch to divert the water to the post. Well I guess we must have done something to the beaver's dam. For three days later our water ran out. We rode out to find out why. We followed the ditch back towards the river. And found a big beaver damn across the ditch blocking off our water supply.

The Captain told me to get rid of the beaver dam. Easy job thought I, easy hell! Me and four other fellows could not move any of the logs the beaver built their dam with. I swear they used a pile driver to put those logs in place. I finally had to get a team of mules to break the dam up. Even with a team it was a damn hard job. Well we got it broken up, and the water started flowing to the post. Would you believe that the very next night the beavers built another dam! And the water stopped flowing! We went back and tore out the second dam. The beavers left. The little buggers moved a mile up the ditch and built another dam. This dam was bigger than the previous two dams combined.

I thought I will need dynamite to shift this dam. We were all set to blow up the dam. When a Game Warden came up, and told me I could not blow up the dam. And if I did, I would be in big trouble. "Can I trap the beavers?" I asked. "No!" was the reply. "Could I shoot the beavers?" "Hell no!" he shouted at me. "Well what can I do?" He said, "You can find another source of water. The beavers, and their dam stays." I thought here I am in the west. I chased Indians, cattle, rustlers, and all kinds of people while guarding the Rio Grande borders and damn beavers beat the U.S. Army.

There are all kinds of wildlife in Utah. Must be thousands of hummingbirds, bobcats, wild dogs, and bears, you name it is out here. At one time the government moved a bunch of Indians out of this area. The Indians left their dogs behind. Indians always had lots of dogs in their camps. Anyway these dogs would come roaming around the garbage cans on post. Looking for something to eat, fighting and raising hell while doing it. During the day they lived in holes in the ground.   Also living in holes in the ground were prairie dogs, thousands and thousands of them. They stand on their hind legs in front of their hole, and look all around. They can see the slightest movement. If you raise your rifle to shoot them, pop, down the hole they go. There are these prairie dog holes all over her, and many a horse have stumbled into one of these holes. Some even breaking their leg and ended up being shot.

It was out here we would hunt long eared jackrabbits while on horseback. Lots of jackrabbits and very big, one of these fellows could feed four people. At Fort Duchesne there is not a town. It is seventy-two miles to the nearest railroad line. Speaking of railroads reminds me of the story about this fellow, who was a witness to a railroad crash.

Seems like there was a terrible crash between two trains, the railroad officials came to town to find out what happened. They asked around if anyone had seen the crash. One fellow came forward and said, "I saw exactly what happened." "Tell us what happened!" demanded the railroad officials. The old boy said, "Well I was riding up on the ridge outside of town a little ways. I looked to my left, and saw a train coming down the tracks. I looked to my right, and I saw another train coming down the same track. And they were both heading for one another." "What did you do?" asked the railroad officials. "Do?" said the old boy, "I didn't do anything." "Didn't you ride down and try and stop the train?" asked the railroad officials. "No." he said. "Did you think anything at all?" asked the railroad people. "Yes I thought of something." he replied. "Well what did you think?" asked the railroad officials. The old boy replied, "I was thinking this is a hell of a way to run a railroad."

I left Fort Du Chesnee in a buckboard pulled by two mules, to get a railroad connection. I had to sit on a wooden slat for seventy-two miles. Let me tell you that was a fun ride. Two days out we stopped at the Stagecoach Hotel.

63

Someone told me about this buckboard trip. It went over the side of the pass, and killed the people in it. I said to the driver, "Does the buckboard go over the side of the pass much?" The driver replied, "Only once."

The owner of the hotel said, "Well what will you have for dinner?" I said, "What do you have?" "Well we don't get as many people coming in like we used to. Some days we had as many as four or five people a day. Now we only get one or two. You can have jerked beef and biscuits." "Fine with me, how much?" "Oh three dollars will cover it," he said. "Little steep isn't it?" I said. "Depends on how hungry you are," he replied. Needless to say I had no choice. So I had jerked beef and biscuits. I got to my railway connection, it was a COG railway. That took you over the mountain to connect with the main line, and caught a train to Denver, Colorado.

Chapter 25

All I had was twenty cents

Now think about this! I was waiting for the train coming from the west coast that would be taking me to Philadelphia. Here I was in Denver. I had two hundred and twenty dollars in twenty-dollar gold pieces in my pocket and a check for six hundred dollars. I had not had a drink in three years while I was in Utah. I was feeling on top of the world. In comes the train with many sleeping cars on it. The train stopped here for only twenty minutes. I had my baggage all checked in and was ready to go.

A bunch of men came running off the train and asked me, "Where can we get some whiskey?" This was a special troop train full of soldiers. These soldiers saw duty in China, Philippines, and Hawaii Territory. Now just think what happened to me in twenty minutes. I knew some of these fellows, and they talked me into having a drink with them. Well they got their whiskey and plenty of it and me right along with them. It took me about ten minutes or so to get fired up. And after a few hours of drinking on the train, I was in fine shape.

I do not think half the boys on the train knew where they were. They did not care, and had plenty of money to burn. I remember I was drunk most of the time. And me and some other fellows got off the train in Harrisburg, Pennsylvania to get some whiskey. We came back to the train, but the train left without us. We went back in town and just kept on drinking. We all ended getting thrown in jail for the night. The next day they let us all out of jail. And I caught the next train to Philadelphia. I was feeling so bad I did not care if I lived or died.

When I got to Philadelphia I put my hand in my pockets, and all I could come up with was twenty cents. No gold pieces, no baggage claim check, no six-hundred dollar check. All I had was twenty cents. I figured what the hell! I might as well get a drink. Well I walked into the nearest saloon. And there were some of the soldier boys I had been on the train with. They were whoop-

ing it up and having a good time. All of a sudden, a fellow walked up to me and said, "Hey Jess here is your baggage claim tickets, and your six-hundred dollar check." I did not know this man, and I did not recognize him. But I was awful damn glad to see him. I spent over two-hundred dollars on the train, some spent all they had. It took five days to get from Denver to Philadelphia. I remember the conductor saying, "Now boys give me your tickets because if I don't get them now, I will never get them."

I wanted to get my check cashed. But I needed someone to identify me. I found a fireman that I knew from Twelfth and Reed Streets, and he helped me get my check cashed. My fireman friend took four-hundred dollars off me, and told me to pick it up later. I had two-hundred dollars and did me and the boys make a night of it. You bet we did!

We went from saloon to saloon all night long. The next day I was broke. I went and picked up my four hundred dollars, and had another hell of a good time. The money lasted about seven days. While in Philadelphia I went to see my brother and he told me, "You cannot drink in my house." I said, "Hell with you! And hell with your house!" and walked out. Here I was broke for sure. Had a hangover, and did not know what to do. I thought what the hell. I will join up in the Army again.

I went to the Recruiting Office and was told to see some major who was in charge. He said to me, "What did you do with your check?" "I spent it," says I. He said, "I do not know how you could have cashed that check without my signature on it." "Well I did and here I am." He said, "Do you know you could have taken a trip to Europe and had a good time." I said, "I took a nice trip from Denver to Philadelphia, and had a good time." He said, "You soldiers just go crazy when you get some money! I guess you want to come home now?" I said, "Yes Sir." The major turned to the sergeant who was there and said, "Have him fill out the forms." Fill out the forms! Hell! I was so sick and tired and hung over, I could not even write my own name.

The major said, "Sergeant let him practice writing his name for awhile." Well finally, the forms were completed, and I signed them. I do not know if the major completed them or the sergeant did. I had a good time coming from Den-

ver to Philadelphia, and a good time while I was in Philadelphia. I did not have a good time in Utah, not having a drink in three years. So it just goes to prove if you do not have drink once in awhile, you could end up miserable.

Chapter 26

Meowing Like Cats

I was sent to Fort Slocum, New York, to train new recruits. I nearly went out of my mind training these recruits. Drilling was not too bad. It was when they got out of line, but there were ways to take care of that.

You have a corporal or sergeant in each squad room .The squad room is a big room that sleeps about two hundred men. There is also a poolroom and a reading room. In the squad room, the lights go off at nine each night, and the reading room off at eleven.

My boys thought they would have a little fun with me. They were throwing shoes across the room and meowing like cats. I told them to be quiet a few times, but they would not listen. Well the next night I crept up to the squad room and they were carrying on again. I slipped inside real quiet, threw on the light switch, and asked who has been making all the noise. No one said a word, no one moved. Some were under the blankets with their heads covered. I told them to all get up, get dressed and go down to the beach in full gear.

Their gear was already cleaned for tomorrow's inspection, and the little walk on the beach meant they would have to clean it again. I doubled timed them up and down the beach for thirty minutes. I then took them back to the squad room, and told them if I hear any more noise, I would double-time them for two hours. I did not hear a peep out of anyone.

There are two ways of handling trouble troops. Let them take care of themselves, or throw them in the Hoosegow. You see it was six men who were causing all the problems. Four of these men got beaten up pretty bad, and the other two took a hint pretty quick, no more trouble.

I hated working with recruits, but I loved escort duty. Escort duty was when you escorted the new recruits to their new posts, usually Texas or Colorado. The government would have an entire train and send one sergeant and two corporals as escorts. Of course, if you did not have any money, you did not have a good time.

In the seven months I was at Fort Slocum, I made three trips to Wyoming, two to Texas, and two to California. You would take the troops to their new post, lay over a day, raise hell in town in town and head back to Fort Slocum. That was good duty. In those days, you could always find someone to borrow money from. The going rate was borrow five and pay back six. This was expensive, but I borrowed at this rate and had a hell of a good time on escort duty.

Chapter 27
Leaning over about 35 degrees

One time I was Wagon Master for the Army Signal Corps. And I was taking a wagon to Chickamauga, Tennessee. I was fully in charge of the wagon train, and could hire and fire who I pleased.

Let me tell you, I was a damn good Mule Skinner. As a Mule Skinner I had to break mules to the wagon. This is no easy job but I got it done. I rode in the saddle on the nigh (left) mule. The lead mule had an iron bar running from his breast strap, to the breast strap off the other mules. When I jerked on the lead mule, he would turn left. When I pulled on the line, the mule would turn right. Whatever way the lead mule went the others had to follow because of the iron bar. It is just like you were pushing the mules around with your hands.

I used to take a lot of big shots out to see the area. I would use a wire reel wagon hitched to four mules. I had the honor of driving some Generals: Greely, Brooke, Wheeler, and Grant Jr., all around Lookout Mountain and Missionary Ridge.

I was with the Signal Corps about two months in Tennessee, when they got orders to pull out. I cannot remember where they were going to. But I got into an argument with one of the Signal Corps Sergeants. Told him to go to hell, and I upped and quit.

I ended up with the First City Troop Cavalry in Virginia, and left on 28 July 1898. On the U.S. transport Massachusetts heading to Porto Rico. On the ship was The First City Troop Philadelphia Cavalry. On 3 August 1898, we were almost into Ponce, Porto Rico. When the ship ran aground on a coral reef, we were about four miles out from Ponce. Traveling about twenty knots an hour when the ship hit the reef. Boys did the ship stop quick. She was leaning over about thirty-five degrees. Of course everyone was a little shaken up.

General Miles was on the beach at Ponce, but not for long. Out comes a little steamboat with General Miles on it. He got close enough to yell, "Get them horses off the boat! Put a sling on them and drop them in the water!" Funny thing the Cavalrymen from the other side of the boat that was listing over, ran to the other side of the boat to try and upright it. Needless to say it did not work.

A big steel cable was hooked onto the ship. From the cruiser Columbia in an attempt to pull us offs the reef. All of a sudden, the cable snapped, and wrapped itself around the propeller of the ship Columbia. A diver went down to get it untangled. In the meantime we were unloading the horses. There was a lot of little steamboats rounding up the horses, and heading them for the beach. They had a hard time rounding up the horses. It took a few days to get all the horses off. Hot as hell and many of the horses died from the heat. I was in Ponce but could not find my outfit. So I lay down to take a rest.

Pretty soon a Cavalry Troop started setting up their camp close by me. I walked over to a man and said, "I can't find my outfit. Can you give me something to eat?" "Certainly." he said. When I saw what he was putting on my plate. I thought this must be a hotel outfit. Roast pork, butter cream cakes, and good coffee. I thought to myself, this is an outfit I would like to be with. Just then a man came over and said, "Can you cook?" I said, "Only what I learned in the Army." "Well you are the man we need. How would you like to join up with us?" "Hell yes!" I said. "When can you start?" he asked. "As soon as I get my gear together!" I said. Getting my gear together took me about five minutes. "What is your name?" He asked me. "Jack." I said. I asked this fellow what his name was and he said, "Just call me Percy."

A short time later a man walked up to me and asked, "Where is Mr. Biddle?" I told him I did not know a Mr. Biddle. He said, "Who is the man cooking with you?" I said, "Percy." I thought this was funny. So I asked another fellow, "Is Percy of Bailey, Banks, and Biddle?" He said, "Yes." I said, "Got some big shots in this outfit." He said, "Oh, I don't know."

At supper Percy said, "Mr. Glendenning you serve the meat. Mr. Walker the coffee, and Jack you serve the bread and gravy." Mr. Glendenning was the man I asked who Percy was. Mr. Glendenning and his brother were here. They were both big bankers from Philadelphia, at Third and Chestnut streets. A Captain Groome was the Commanding Officer. Captain Groome was the man who started the Pennsylvania State Police.

Percy told me when he was away, I was in charge. No one got anything unless I Ok'd it. We had everything in the store tent. Whiskey, wine, Belfast Water, ginger ale, cakes of all kinds, cigars, cigarettes, and pipe tobacco. They had a private yacht bring all this stuff in for them. I thought this is one hell of a way to fight a war.

While we were in Porto Rico, we camped at a lumberyard for a week. I found a Spanish baker, and we had fresh bread and rolls every day. We also had fresh milk delivered to us. There was this man who would drive his cows out to the lumberyard, and milk them on the spot. We boiled the milk before we drank it.

The Philadelphia Cavalry was the bodyguard of General Brooke. General Brooke was the big shot of the whole operation in Puerto Rico. I got up early in the morning to make coffee. I had plenty of company as we would have Coffee Royal (coffee and whiskey). This was one of the best jobs I ever had as far as work was concerned. These men I was with must have had a lot of money, and underwear. They all wore silk underwear. They did not bother to wash the underwear, and they just threw it away when it was dirty. Well the war did not last long a few shots were fired. The next thing I know, I was on a boat heading for the United States aboard the U.S. Transport Mississippi.

Chapter 28

Are you the City Troop Cook?

To kill time on the way back most of the Philadelphia Cavalry fellows would match ten, and twenty gold dollar pieces. I could only watch as I could not afford to play. The outfit got a big purse up. And offered it to the engine room crew, if the crew got us back to the States in quick time. We were due to dock in Jersey City, New Jersey. Well the engine room crew got their purse as we made good time to the States.

We got off the boat in Jersey City, and was loaded on a train going to Philadelphia. The train pulled into Broad and Washington Street Station. You should have seen all the fine horses, and carriages there to pick up the boys of the Philadelphia Cavalry. The outfit was going to a hotel for a big breakfast banquet. I was detailed to guard the baggage. So I sat down and waited.

I was sitting there all dirty, and in my old clothes when a man walked up to me and said, "Are you the City Troop Cook?" "Yes." says I. He said, "There is a nice big carriage out there, with two ladies sitting in it. I walked over and said, "Ladies, I can't go anywhere with you. I am in old clothes, and too dirty." They said, "Nonsense! You are going to the breakfast banquet with us! So get in the carriage." Well I got in the carriage, and away we went to breakfast.

We got to the hotel and I walked in with one lady on each arm. Inside all the City Troop was dressed if full dress uniform. And here I was in full dress dirt. I was shown a table and I sat down to eat, the ladies standing either side of my chair. Every time I reached to get something, they would stop me. And hand me whatever I was reaching for. It got so I could not eat a thing! Damn ladies were making me nervous. After I finished breakfast, the ladies asked me if I wanted to go get my baggage.

You see, all the ladies wanted to be seen with a soldier. I did not have the heart to tell them I was a civilian. We left in the fine carriage and went back to the train. Picked up my baggage, and I was taken to a hotel at Twenty- Third and Chestnut Street. I had a nice room. Took a bath, changed my clothes, and went out on the town. I really whooped it up on my night out on the town.

The next morning I saw Captain Groome, and he gave me a letter of introduction to a Mr. Wadner. I told Captain Groome I wanted a job as a trolley car driver. I saw Mr. Wadner, but there were no trolley car drivers' job open. So I thought what the hell. I went into a saloon, and ran into three fellows I knew in the Army. These three had quite a snootful. And asked me to join them for a drink, and that did not take much asking. Well we made time of it that day. Next thing I know, I was back in the Army.

Chapter 29
Guerillas and crocodiles

I left from Camp Mead in Pennsylvania heading for San Francisco, California. At San Francisco I got on a boat heading for the Philippine Islands. On the way to the Philippines we stopped at Honolulu, Hawaiian Territory, and Japan. I went on a boat called the Tartar. The Tartar was an old English freighter that had seen better days. It took us thirty one days to get from California to the Philippines.

We anchored in Manila Bay Harbor about two thirds of a mile from the beach. We were put in a little steamboat that took us to the beach. As we neared the beach, we were told to jump overboard and wade the rest of the way to the beach. As the steamboat could only go so far in. From the beach we were marched to a place called the Walled City. This is where our barracks were. They called them barracks, we called them swimming holes. The barracks were a bamboo hut built on stilts out over the water. We stayed in these huts a few days, and moved up to the front lines. The front line was out in the jungle. My outfit was detailed to pull guard duty.

Where I was out in the jungle having to worry about swamps, crocodiles, and native guerilla fighters. It is times like this I ask myself, "What the hell are you doing out here?" It seemed like every place I went to, I had something to worry about. Out on the plains it was Indians, snakes, mountain lions, and what have you. Here in the Philippine jungle it was guerillas, crocodiles, and lord knows what else.

When we pulled guard duty we had six men and a Corporal of the Guard. Two men would stand duty for two hours on, and four off, for a twenty-four hour period. Out in the jungle you did not walk your tour of duty. You and the other guard stood back to back. So you could see in all directions. Out here it was a thick jungle. And the natives could crawl through the tall grass, and throw a Bolo Knife at you. Or sneak up and cut your throat. Sometimes we were sent to guard a certain road. When we performed this type of duty, you performed this duty by yourself. Let me tell you, this guerilla warfare is bad. You see, you do not know where the enemy native is. A native may walk right by you and be ok. Or he could go by you, sneak out in the bush, and come back, and slit your throat.

One night we were on the Island of Luzon. The Thirteenth Infantry was camped nearby us. About two in the morning a Sentry Guard heard a lot of noise in the bush. He thought it was some natives coming after him. He let go a few shots in the direction of the noise. All the soldiers jumped up half asleep running around wondering what was happening. Next thing we knew, a herd of about twenty water buffaloes came charging through the camp. Many of the soldiers were injured by the buffalo some pretty seriously. The Sentry caught hell from the colonel. As for me, I was ok. And glad it was not the guerillas attacking us. This incident took place on the Island of Luzon at a place called the Water Works.

Next we went to the Island of Panay. We crossed this Island from one end to the other. Why we did this, I do not know. We had about eighteen hundred men in our outfit, and we had to transport our gear by Water Buffalo carts. What a hell of a time we had doing this. The carts were hard to learn how to drive. They were made out of wood, with big tall wooden wheels. The cart was hitched to two water buffalo bulls. You would poke the bull with a stick and shout "Yus, Yus, Yus." The old bulls would travel along at a pretty good pace. And then for no reason, would stop dead in their tracks. And then all of a sudden, off they would go again, and then stop again. Every so often you would have to unhitch the bulls, to let them roll in the mud. The natives said if we did not this the bulls would go crazy. In my opinion they did not have far to go. For some unknown reason we would only travel at night.

Well this one night the bull I was driving must have gone crazy as he was running at a hell of a clip. We rode across a bridge, and when we got to the other side someone said, "Who fell off?" "Must have been Jimmy." someone said. "Pass the word up the line, man fell off bridge." The word came back down, "Look for him." Some of the fellows dove in the water. And after a little while we found Jimmy. He must have hit his head, as it was all cut open. We put Jimmy in the cart, and pushed on.

Next morning after a breakfast of rice, and coffee, we buried Jimmy. We put a little marker on his grave, and left. It was the same thing day in day out crossing this island.

Chapter 30

Loaded our pistols with Dum Dum bullets

Only some of the fellows went crazy from drinking a local drink called Bino. Bino is something like gin. But has a hell of a kick to it.

This one morning we got into a boat, and went to the Island of Cebu. It was on Cebu that an American soldier by the name of Fouse killed a native girl. I think he killed her with a knife. Fouse was locked up in a fort on this island. He was brought to where we were to stand trial for killing this girl. It was common knowledge that there was a plan to let him escape before the trail. But no one would admit this. You see the natives knew Fouse was in our jail. And they expected us to court martial him, and hang him. The plan was for a guard to let Fouse escape to a boat on the beach. And row out to a steamer in the bay that would take him back to the States. The guard on duty was told to tell Fouse of the plan.

One night about ten thirty the guard took Fouse out of his cell to go to the latrine. The guard told Fouse where the boat was, and to make a break for it. The guard waited about twenty minutes and raised the alarm. "Corporal of the Guard prisoner escaped!" Here is the guard running up the road, firing shots, thinking Fouse was on the steamer by now.

A few days later we picked up an American Marine deserter. We found him out in the hills. This deserter was made a colonel in the Philippine Army. Along with this deserter we found Fouse. Fouse ran away as planned. But he took the wrong road. He told me when the guard was firing his rifle he thought he had been set up. And kept going, and eventually ended up with the deserter. A court martial was held, and it lasted for four days. The deserter was hanged. And so was Fouse.

We did not do much on Cebu but lie around and drink Bino. We left Cebu and went to the Island of Samar. To a little town called Borongan. We had some trouble in this town. We were camped at the church about two blocks away was our guardhouse, where we were holding twenty Filipino prisoners. We had gone to bed, and about two in the morning, the church bell was ringing. And some natives came at us from all sides. They fired one volley of shots, and ran away. They were trying to break the prisoners out of the guardhouse. We killed four of the natives and wounded nine. On our side one of the guards was wounded, but no one was killed.

At daylight we got our orders from the Captain, "The sergeant is going to give you some prisoners. Take them to the beach and make sure they don't come back." These prisoners we were to take to the beach had killed some of our boys in a previous fight. We all knew what we had to do. We loaded our pistols with Dum Dum bullets. Marched the prisoners down to the beach, and shot them in the back of the head. After we shot them, we had other Filipino prisoner's weight them down with rocks. Take them out in the ocean, and dump their bodies.

As I said before, we could not tell who the enemy was but we had ways of making them talk. We used two methods. One was the water treatment. You would sit the prisoner in a chair. Tie up his hands and legs. Force his head back. Open his mouth, and pour water down his throat. If he tightened his throat up to try and stop the water from going down, we would hit him on the side of his neck. We would keep pouring water down his throat until his stomach puffed out. When his stomach was full of water, we would ask our questions. If he did not answer, we would kick him in the stomach. Some would talk, and some would not.

Another thing we did was to take a piece of cord, and a piece of wood. Make a tourniquet, and place it around the man's balls. Boys this was an awful thing to do. Sometimes you would nearly cut their balls off by this method.

When the natives got hold of ours, they did similar things. A tribe called the Igorots did this. I am not too proud of some of the things I did in the Philippines. These Igorots did a dance called the Kanao. The men dressed in feathered headdress. Carried a spear, and would dance in a line to the rhythm of beaten sticks. At the front of the line was a man carrying a pole. At the top of the pole was the head of a person they killed. They would dance and shout jabbing the pole in the air. They also brushed the ground with the feet and hands of the person they killed. As if they were using a broom. They would bury the head dig it up later, and a warrior would use it to decorate his hut. These Igorots were tough customers. It was said they would torture themselves using our methods, in order to toughen themselves up.

We had Krag-Jorgenson rifles with sharp point bullets. These bullets could go through two feet of oak. These Igorots would charge you with a Bolo knife in one hand, and a spear or dagger in the other. It has been known for Igorots to have three bullets put in him and keep coming at you. The natives had other methods of killing you. They would dig a hole in the ground. Sharpen some bamboo poles to a sharp point. And rig the bamboo into a spring like affair. If someone fell in the hole it would trigger the spring, and the bamboo would slice through your body. They also made small cannons out of bamboo rods. And empty salmon cans. They would load this homemade cannon. With bits of rocks, iron pieces or what have you, and fire it. Its range was about a city block. But if it hit you, it would kill, or cripple you. They would also creep around at night, and stab you through the slats of your bamboo hut.

Chapter 31

Guarding the Paymaster Ship

I was assigned to guard the Paymasters Ship along with some other fellows. The ships name was the Philadelphia. We went from island to island paying the troops. We would pull into an island and be met by a guard detail. We would grab sacks of money. In the sacks were five, ten, and twenty-dollar gold pieces, and pass them over to the guard detail. The government had been paying the troops with gold for a year and a half. Until they found out what the Chinamen were doing.

Seems like some Chinamen were putting the gold shipment together, they would knock the bags of gold against each other. This would knock some of the gold dust off the coins. And the Chinamen would pocket the gold dust. In addition to the money, we also took food, and clothing to the troops scattered around the islands.

One day we were off the coast of Ormac, and there was a Gun Boat on the island of Luzon waiting to escort us. On this particular day we had a lot of money on the Philadelphia. The Paymaster and his clerk went to the town to see the Quartermaster. The Paymaster told us to stay on the Philadelphia and wait for him. Well suppertime came around, no Paymaster, no clerk.

It was a nice evening and we were on the deck shooting the breeze. The Captain said, "I do not see the Gun Boat." Then he looked at the barometer and said, "Holy Hell!" He yelled to his crew "Let's get out of here!" He told us to go in the Wheelhouse, and brace ourselves. The Captain was tied to the wheel.

All of a sudden, it got dark and started raining to beat the band. Then the wind started tossing our little ship around. Up and down, side to side. Things were being thrown all around the wheelhouse, dishes, glasses, things crashing all around us.

We could hear the fireman shouting, "Water coming in the engine room." The captain shouting, "Stay with it!" In the meantime us poor buggers is getting thrown all over the cabin. The Captain was trying to get the ship out of the harbor, and ride the storm out on the seas. We only needed to go about half a mile. It took us a very long time to make this half mile.

The storm was so bad it tore up the underwater telephone cables to China. Soon we saw the lights of the Gun Boat. It was looking for us. They thought we had sunk. At daybreak all was calm, and we went back into the harbor.

The poor Paymaster was going crazy. He thought we had sunk with all the money on board. You see the Paymaster is not supposed to be off the Ship. He could have been court-martialed.

Chapter 32

Massacre of the Ninth Infantry

My next tour of duty was on the Island of Samar. Samar is the island where the Ninth Infantry was cut up, eighty-four men. Bellies cut open, eyes jabbed out, fingers, and also their privates cut off. Some of their faces were also chopped up. I was told the story of how it happened.

This attack happened during the time of the Boxer Rebellion. Some of the Ninth Infantry went to Japan and some were sent to the Island of Samar. Shortly after the massacre of the Ninth Infantry, I landed at a place called Basey. The attack happened in a place called Balangia.

Captain Waters was the Commander of the Ninth Infantry. And many of his men were lost in the jungle. Some of the men went blind from little worms in their eyes, and many men had gone mad. Captain Waters kept going out looking for his men. The camp Surgeon told Captain Waters not to go out in the jungle, as Captain Waters was very sick. Although sick he had guts. He went out and found some of his troops. One day he ended up in Balangia, and he set up camp there.

One day the Mayor of Balangia asked Captain Waters if the villagers could cut the grass around the church. As the villagers were having a funeral the next morning, Captain Waters gave his permission. The next morning at six, the villagers carried a coffin into the church, and started to cut the grass with their Bolo knives. At six the soldiers went to breakfast. The Surgeon and Captain Waters were still asleep in their tent. Inside the church were some of the men and women attending the funeral service. But there was no body in the coffin. It was full of Bolo Knives.

Outside one of the villagers asked the guard at the church the time he told him, "Seven." As soon as the guard said that, the man split the guard's head with his Bolo knife. This was a signal for the other village men to take action.

The soldiers who went to breakfast did not take their weapons with them, and were caught off guard. The soldiers were outnumbered ten to one. The villagers started killing the soldiers. Captain Waters and the Surgeon were murdered in their tent. The bugler was blowing to arms. But he was soon killed. The cook took a baseball bat, and it was said he killed nine natives with the bat. The cook and nine others escaped in an outrigger boat, and paddled to the American Garrison at Leyte Island to raise the alarm.

If only the soldiers had not left their guns behind in their tents. They would have had a much better chance. The soldiers were buried in a big trench. I think the boys from the gunboat buried the dead. We were sent to find the people who attacked the Ninth Infantry boys. At each little place we stopped we were told the same story. I do not know.

This one day we were camped at a little town beside a graveyard. It was not a graveyard as you and I know. It was very different from anything I ever saw. The graveyard was a wall about eight feet deep with a lot of little holes in it. In the holes a coffin was slid in, and the hole was sealed with a piece of glass. So the relatives could see the person in the coffin. They have to pay so much a month to the Mayor of the village, to keep the coffin in the wall. If you did not pay the coffin was taken out. And the body was thrown on a heap with the others, whose families was unable to pay the monthly rent. I have seen as many as four to five hundred skulls just lying in a big pile.

One night at this graveyard we were attacked by some of the natives. They fired a few shots and ran away. Luckily no one was hit. Next day we got orders to go to the town of Basey, and relieve a company of Marines. About two in the morning we were attacked again no one was injured. Later that morning we went to see the Mayor of the village. To try to find out who attacked us. We had a native to act as interpreter.

The Mayor was a big fat man dressed in a white suit. The Captain told the interpreter, "Ask him who shot at us." The Mayor replied, "The men who shot you are on the island over there." pointing to an island. We looked and saw tiny trees. No one could hide on this island, as there was nowhere to hide. The

Captain turned to us and said, "Give this big shot the works." So the Mayor was marched down to the beach. And some shots were pumped into him, and he was thrown into the sea.

When we came back the Captain said, "Burn the village." There were about seventy-five bamboo shacks in the village. And we set them all on fire as the Captain told us to do. Soon the sky was lit up and full of smoke. The village we set on fire was close to Leyte. Where out in the harbor was an American Gun Boat. The Captain of the ship sent word he wanted to talk to our Commanding Officer. We found out later our Captain told the Gun Boat Commander the natives had set their village on fire and tried to blame it on the Americans.

Well things got quiet on the islands so we just lie around drinking Bino and go swimming. Soon word came through the war was over and we were going home. We boarded a ship for the United States. We stopped at Japan, and the Hawaiian Islands, and then into San Francisco. I served three years and three months in the Philippines.

Chapter 33

Gassed

My next assignment was to the Third Artillery until World War I broke out. I was transferred to Battery C of the Twelfth Artillery, and was sent to Verdun, France. We were to train the French on our seventy-five millimeter guns. We were told the troops at Verdun had not fired a shot in nine months. I had been in France about two months, and I had two hours of fighting. One day we got orders to fire on the Germans. It got hot and heavy there for a while. Next thing I know we got orders to pull out, so we did. I was headed for Belleau Woods.

The End of Jesse's entries.

Chapter 34

Grandson's Closing Words

Jesse's diary ends here. He was gassed on June 22, 1918 at Beaulieu Woods in France, while on the Expeditionary Forces on the Spring Drive of 1918 during WWI. He was hospitalized in the U.S. Army Hospital #9 Lakewood, New Jersey. He was diagnosed as having pleuritic adhesions following emphysema and pneumonia. On 11 December 1918, he was discharged from the Army while in the hospital. When he was discharged from the hospital, he was given $161.46 and a train ticket from Lakewood, New Jersey to Philadelphia, Pennsylvania. He returned to the Army the following items:

One bag
One belt
Three Chevrons (stripes)
Two ornaments
One cord
1 pair of gloves
One pair of breeches
One pair of leggings
One coat
One poncho
One pair of drawers
One undershirt
Three stockings
One overcoat
One hat
One shirt
One pair of shoes

His Military career was over. There is no doubt in my mind he led a colorful life. I only wish I could have recorded all his adventures. I remember attending his funeral in Philadelphia, he had a Military Funeral. The flag on his casket was presented to my Grandmother and Funeral Guards fired three shots over his grave. He died on 12 September 1944.

Names Jesse C. Davisson
served under
Henry C. Hays
John R. Day

Henry C. Hays

Private Troop G 7th Cavalry

Fairmont Recruiting Station, Fairmont Ave Philadelphia, Pa *turned away for service*

Enlisted 26 January 1893 Camden, N.J

Discharged 25 April 1896 at Fort Apache, Arizona

Enlisted 3 May 1896 at Fort Apache, Arizona

Discharged 19 March 1898 Fort Apache, Arizona *Dishonorable discharge*

Jesse/Jack/John/Henry/name unknown

April / May 1898 to June / July 1898

Wagon Master, Muleskinner, Army Signal Corps

En-route taking a wagon to Chickamauga, Tennessee

Argued with a Corps Signal Sergeant and left his position, headed to Philadelphia

Jack/other—Wrote down he gave false name as a volunteer when mustered into service

Spanish War

July 1898

First City Troop Philadelphia Cavalry

Volunteer

July 1898 mustered into Federal Service
Horseman, Saddler, City Troop Cook
August 1898
U.S. Transport Massachusetts sailed at noon 28 July 1898 Newport News, Virginia
Arrived off the coast of Porto Rico August 3, 1898
Spanish War ended sent back to United States
U.S. Transport Mississippi
Docked 10 September Jersey City, New Jersey
Took train to Philadelphia and attended City Troop function
September 1898 Philadelphia, mustered out of Federal Service
Stayed in Philadelphia until March 1899

Jesse C. Davisson and John R. Day
Jesse Davisson *enlisted with this name and discharged
John R. Day *enlisted with this name and discharged
Jesse obtained papers of enlistment and discharge with both names
Private Company F 19th Infantry Casual Detachment
Enlisted 19 May 1899 Philadelphia, Pa
Discharged 24 June 1902 Fort McDowell, California
Expiration term of service
Served 3 years

John R. Day
11th Infantry
20 April 1904 – 27 May 1904
Desertion
*It is speculated that Jesse served time for his desertion
Leavenworth Military Prison
All records were destroyed at National Army Records in the fire of 1970
St. Louis, Missouri

John R. Day
Private Troop H 1st Cavalry
To serve three years
Enlisted 23 January 1908 Jefferson Barracks St. Louis, Missouri

Discharged 22 January 1911
Honorably discharged
Expiration of term of service

John R. Day
Private/Corporal Company C 2nd Regiment of Infantry
Said John R. Day was born in St Louis, Missouri. Enlisted age was said to be
37yrs old
To serve three years
Enlisted 19 February 1911 Fort Slocum, New York
3 March 1911 Recruit Depot: John R. Day. Fourth recruit Company G.S.J.
Shall discharge duty of Corporal by Commanding Officers of the 14th and 12th
Cavalry
Shall discharge duty of Corporal in Company L, Second Regiment of Infantry
20 February 1912
Jesse was a Sergeant June 1912
Four months later in October 1912 he was a private
AWOL 2 days, 30 October 1912 to 1 November 1912
Shall discharge the duties of Corporal 13 August 1913
He went AWOL in November 1913 after that no promotions above Private
AWOL 2 days, 9 November 1913 to 11 November 1913
Discharged 23 February 1914 Recruit Depot Fort McDowell, California
*Expiration of term of service
Said John R. Day was born in St Louis, Missouri. Enlisted age was said to be
37yrs old

Jesse C. Davisson
Third Artillery
WW1 transferred to outfit below
Saddler of Battery C 12th Field Artillery
Army serial number: 128786
Enlisted 14 March 1914 Fort Myer, Virginia
Age of 51 *written on papers
Was to serve 7 years
Sailed from U.S. 10 February 1914
The Battle for Belleau Woods: June 4—July 10, 1918

American Expeditionary Forces (AEF)

Assignment: Train troops on the latest 75mm guns, Verdun

Arrived at Chateau-Thierry 2 June 1918

On 22 June 1918 Jesse was gassed at Chateau-Thierry

American Expeditionary Forces (AEF) January 1918-September 1918 Spring Drive 1918

Aisne-Marne Sector, 75 miles North East of Paris

In a Triangular area bounded by Chateau-Thierry, Soissons and Reims

Chateau-Thierry, Belleau Woods. Flanders Front, Verdun Sector

Arrived at port on return to U.S. 29 August 1918

Discharged 11 December 1918 at 9th General Hospital Lakewood, New Jersey

Physical disability: Per 3rd Ind. HQ. E.D. November 25, 1918

Cause of disability: Plevritis adhesions following emphysema and pneumonia

In line of duty Disability 10/10 old job ¼ new job permanent.

*As shown on papers of discharge at Hospital

Military Installations

The primary reason for stationing troops in the west was to control the Indians. Posts were established to protect seacoasts, and to guard international frontiers. Mexico established posts in Texas to block illegal movement of persons and goods from the United States into its territory. Spain and France maintained their petty garrisons, face to face on either side of the Arroyo (a watercourse or creek in an arid region) Hondo. For the United States the period of the Mexican War and, more particularly, the Civil War saw large numbers of troops in the west engaged in doing something other than controlling the Indians. Yet the great majority of Western Military Posts established prior to the Spanish-American War, regardless of their initial purpose, were concerned with Indians.

Where troops were stationed, facilities to accommodate them came into existence, more often than not erected by the labor of the troops themselves. The sites for most posts, even overnight encampments, were chosen with care. Need, either real or assumed was an initial consideration for those posts intended to be maintained for any length of time. Water was essential, and without exception, western forts were built close to what was considered a dependable source, usually a stream, but occasionally a spring or lake. As long as posts were constructed by the labor of the soldiers, a supply of suitable material, not too inconveniently located was necessary. Workable stone, timber, earth from which adobes (a building made of sun-dried bricks made from earth and straw) could be fashioned into, or a little lean type of affair called a Jacale, made from brush was also used. Physically, at least in its early years a Western Military Post was very much a product of its environment.

Military Installations had many different names: There were agencies, arsenals, barracks, batteries, blockhouses, camps, cantonments, depots, sub-depots, forts, military prisons, posts, sub-posts, picket-posts, presidios, stations, and at least one stockade and one redoubt. Some of the terms are self-explanatory, or so it would seem, yet in actual practice many were applied in such a manner as to destroy their specific meaning. The designation arsenal, battery and military prison were used with reasonable exactness. The term agency was applied to a garrison maintained in connection with an Indian Agency, while the term station usually referred to a garrison located at stations on the mail or telegraph routes. As used (Standing Rock Agency, Plum Creek Station), those were actually place names. Barracks in theory, were centers in which troops were located temporarily until they could be reassigned. Jefferson Barracks existed for one hundred and twenty years. During that period it performed almost every function that might be demanded of a military post, yet it was always designated a barracks. Depots were centers for the storage and distribution of supplies. Sub-depots, though completely separate posts were subordinate to depots. Arsenals, barracks, and depots were often associated with other posts for example: Fort Union (New Mexico) and Fort Union Arsenal were located on the same Military Installation, Fort Whipple and Prescott Barracks were immediately adjacent, and for a time Benica (California) consisted of Benica Barracks, Benica Arsenal, Benica Subsistence Depot and Benica Quartermaster Depot. Posts designated batteries, blockhouses, sub-posts, and picket posts were invariably subordinate to other posts.

The problem of nomenclature becomes even more confused in the cases of camps, cantonments, forts and posts. To begin with, post is a generic term including by definition, all positions at which troops are stationed. Hence, a fort, barracks, or arsenal, agency, camp and so on, is also a post. Examples of this are: Posts on the Limpia, post in the Navajo country, new post near Fort Hall, and a post at El Paso. Many of the posts established by the United States prior to the Civil War, and some thereafter, were simply referred to by name of the location they occupied. The establishment in 1817, of what was to become Fort Snelling ushered in a period when the tendency to call all new posts, cantonments. This practice had nothing to do with the presumed permanence of a post. The designation became so common that by 1881 there were, west of the Mississippi River, three forts one barracks and four cantonments. By definition, a cantonment is an impermanent establishment, yet the cantonments so called were not intended to be temporary. To correct this anomaly, general adjutant General Roger Jones issued orders number eleven on 6 February 1832, providing that:

1. It is the order of the Secretary of War that all military posts designated cantonments be hereafter called forts, and that the works of old point comfort be called Fort Monroe and not Fortress Monroe.

2. All new posts, which may be hereafter established, will receive their names from the War Department, and be announced in general orders from the headquarters of the Army.

3. Officers and other concerned will take due notice of the above orders and govern accordingly.

Despite the order of 1832 providing that all new posts would receive their names from the War Department, the sources for the names of the forts continued to vary. The officer who established them, others by the officers who ordered their establishments, still others by the general in command of the Army and some by the Secretary of War., named some posts. In very few instances, the names proposed initially were rejected by the War Department. Many posts underwent one or more changes of a name as well as designation. An example of this is the Colorado Post, which became Fort Fauntleroy, was renamed Fort Wise and ended up as Fort Lyon. As would be expected, a majority, roughly three fifths of posts were named after Army Officers. All ranks from Second Lieutenant to full General were represented, except that of Lieutenant General. On fort Gratan, Nebraska was named for a brevet (A commission given a military officer higher nominal rank than that for which he receives pay), and one, Mann, Kansas for a Master Teamster. More forts were named for Colonels that for Officers of any other rank, with Brigadier Generals, Major Generals, and Captains following in that order. Only one was named for a full General, Fort Sherman, Idaho in all cases reference is to the rank held at the time the name was first applied to the post, or in the case of deceased officers, the rank at the time of death.

Installations Jesse served or visited

Fort Apache, Arizona

Established 16 May 1870, located south of Mogollon Plateau on the south bank of the east fork of the White River, near the present town of Fort Apache, on what now is the Fort Apache Indian Reservation. Intended to control the Coyotero Apaches, it was situated at the terminus of a military road built into Coyotero Apache country and designed to replace Camp Goodwin. Established by Major Tom Green First U.S. Cavalry. Originally a temporary post known as Camp Ord for Brigadier General O.C. Ord. The name changed to Camp Mogollon on 1 August 1870, then to Camp Thomas for Major General George H. Thomas on 12 September 1870 and to Camp Apache on 2 February 1871. It became a permanent post in 1873, and on 5 April 1879 was designated Fort Apache

Fort Huachuca, Arizona

Pronounced Wha-Chew-Ka. Established 12 February 1877, located at the mouth of Central (post) Canyon, toward the northeast end of the Huachuca Mountains, west of the San Pedro River, and about fifteen miles north of the Mexico border. Fort Huachuca was erected to protect settlers and travelers from the Apache Indians. Established by Captain Samuel M. Whiteside, Sixth U.S. Cavalry, by order of Colonel August V. Kautz, Eighth U.S. Infantry, commanding the department. The post, originally a camp became permanent on 21 January 1878, and was designated a fort in 1882. It saw little activity after the capture of Geronimo, until it became a base of supplies and patrols during the early years of the Mexican Revolution. On 15 February 1949, the post was transferred to the State of Arizona. To be used by the National Guard, and the State Fish and Game Commission. It was reactivated in 1951, deactivated in 1953, and reactivated in February 1954.

Cibicue Creek Battlefield, Arizona

At this place, the engagement took place between the followers of Naka-doklini, a White Mountain Apache Medicine Man. Who had been practicing a new religion, and a Cavalry force under the command of Colonel E.A. Carr on 31 August 1881. The valley at Cibicue Creek is wide and open in contrast to the broken wood terrain on either side. The creek meanders back and forth across it.

San Carlos Agency, Arizona

The San Carlos Agency was established in the Gilla River Valley in 1871. Here, following General Crook's successful campaign in 1872, the Indian Bureau attempted to concentrate most of the Apaches in Arizona and New Mexico. Although many bands were moved to the San Carlos between 1875 and 1878, it remained reasonably content under the administration of agent John Clum. The Apaches never gathered and the attempt failed in the end. Corrupt and insufficient Indian agents, friction between military and civilian authorities, the attempt to make farmers out of wild Indians, and the encroachment of white settlers, kept the reservation in constant turmoil. Renegade bands periodically left for San Carlos, taking refuge in Mexico and raided establishments in Arizona and New Mexico, and skirmished with U.S. troops. After final surrender of Geronimo in 1886, the chief troublemakers were imprisoned in Florida, and most of the remaining Apaches continued to live on either the San Carlos or Fort Apache Reservations to the north.

Fort Clark, Texas

Established 20 June 1852, located on the right side of the Los Moras Creek, near its head at the present town of Bracketville. The post was a link in the frontier defense system and helped guard the San Antonio-El Paso Road. First called Fort Riley, it was designated Fort Clark on 16 July 1852 in honor of Major John B. Clark, 1st U.S. Cavalry who died on 23 August 1847. Established by Captain William Edgar Prince, first U.S. Cavalry, surrendered to the confederacy on 19 March 1861, by order of Brigadier David E. Twiggs. Except for a brief period of confederacy occupancy, the post was not garrisoned again until 10 December 1866, when it was occupied by union troops, commanded by Captain John Wilcox, 4th Cavalry, abandoned in 1946.

Fort Duncan, Texas

Established 28 March 1849, located on the left bank of the Rio Grande River at Eagle Pass. The first permanent building was not erected until 1850. Established by Captain Sidney Burbank, First U.S. Cavalry, the post was named for Colonel John Duncan, Inspector General's Department. Evacuated by Federal Troops on 23 March 1861 by order of Brigadier General David E. Twiggs. Garrisoned during the Civil War by confederate troops re-occupied by Federal Troops on March 23 1868. The site occupied by the post was rented, and for years, the government sought to purchase it, but could not come to an agreement with the owners as to a price. Largely for that reason, the post was abandoned on 31 August 1883. In subsequent years, the department commanders urged reoccupation of the fort, because of its location on one of the main routes of travel into Mexico, and its usefulness in observing and controlling the Rio Grande. In 1891, a cavalry post was established at Eagle Pass, and was the designated post at Eagle Pass or camp at Eagle Pass. Efforts to purchase the site were renewed in 1891, and the government in 1894 finally acquired the site. By this time, the buildings were in ruinous conditions. The post, again called Fort Duncan was occupied irregularly during border troubles with Mexico following the outbreak of the Mexican Revolution. It was permanently abandoned in 1916.

Fort Brown, Texas

Established 28 March 1846, located at the present town of Brownsville, across the Rio Grande from Matamoros, Mexico. Established by Colonel Zachary Taylor, 6th U.S. Infantry just prior to the start of the Mexican War. Construction of the post was made under the direction of Major John Brown, 7th U.S. Infantry, who died 9 May 1846 of wounds received during the Mexican bombardment of the fort. The post was abandoned by order of Brigadier General David E. Twiggs, dated 5 February 1859, and garrison transferred to Fort Duncan, Eagle Pass. Re-occupied on 5 December 1859 because of the activities of Juan Nepomuceno Cortinas along the Mexican border. Evacuated by Union Troops beginning 9 March, and completed 20 March 1861. Occupied by the Confederate until 3 November 1863 when it was evacuated by order of Hamilton P. Bee., Confederate States of America. The town of Brownsville was occupied by the Union Troops on 7 November 1863, but was retaken by the Confederates on 30 July 1864, and was retained by them until the end of the Civil War. On 26 April 1895, the United States government purchased the site. Due to bloodshed and bad feelings between the garrison and the citizens of Brownsville, the post was evacuated in 1906.

Fort Ringwold, Texas

Established 26 October 1848, located on the left bank of the Rio Grande at David's Landing, about half a mile below the Rio Grande City, at the head of Navigation on the river. It was one of the lines of posts established along the Rio Grande, and the western frontier at the close of the Mexican War. Established by Captain Joseph H Lamotte First U.S. Infantry. The initial name was Post at David's Landing, then Camp Ringgold and finally on 16 July 1849, Ringgold Barracks. It was designated Fort Ringgold on 30 December 1878. The post was named for Captain Samuel Ringgold, 3rd U.S. Artillery, who died 11 May 1846 of wounds received in the Battle of Palo Alto. Abandoned on 3 March 1859 by order of Brigadier General David E. Twiggs. The garrison transferred to Camp Hudson. Re-occupied on 9 December 1859 because of the activities of Juan Nepomuceno Cortinas, along the Mexican border. Evacuated by Federal Troops on 7 March 1861, and reoccupied in June 1865. Rebuilt in 1869 on a location a little above the original site, the Federal Government purchased the land occupied by the post in 1881. Abandoned in October 1906 and placed in caretaker status.

Fort Wingate, New Mexico

Established 31 August 1860, located at Ojo Del Oso at the north end of the Zuni Range near the headwaters of the Rio Puerco of the west. Established by Captain William Chapman, 5th U.S. Infantry, named for Colonel Thomas T. Fauntleroy, first U.S. Dragoons. When Fauntleroy resigned to join the Confederacy the post was renamed Fort Lyon on 25 September 1861, for Brigadier General Nathan Lyon, killed 10 August 1861, in the Battle of Wilson's Creek, Missouri. The garrison was withdrawn on 10 September 1861 because of the invasion of New Mexico by Confederate Forces from Texas. A mail station was maintained at the post, and throughout the Civil War was referred to as Fort Fauntleroy in official dispatches. Reoccupied in Jun 1868 by the troops returning, and the Navaho Indians from their imprisonment at Fort Sumner, and by the garrison transferred from Fort Wingate I. The original Wingate was established 22 October 1862 at el Gallo, the Great Spring at San Rafael, abandoned in 1869. It was named for Captain Benjamin Wingate, 5th U.S. Infantry who died 1 June 1862 of wounds received at the Battle of Valverde.

Fort DuChesne, Utah

Utah. Established 20 August 1886, located on a site chosen by Brigadier General Crook, about three miles above the junction of the Du Chesne and Uintah Rivers. Established to control the Uncomphagre, and White River Ute Indians. Who had become restless and resistant to the authority of their agent. Established by Major Fredrick W. Benteen Ninth U.S. Cavalry. The post was ordered abandoned in 1892, but the order was rescinded before it was carried out. Abandoned in 1910, at which time the former post buildings became the Agency Headquarters for the Uintah and Ouray Indian Reservation.

American War Medals
And
Decorations awarded to Jesse

Awards and Decorations
Indian Wars Medal
Spanish War Service Medal
Army of Porto Rico Occupational Medal
Philippine Campaign Medal
Victory Medal WW1 *Aisne Defensive Sector
Good Conduct Medal
Marksmanship Medal

WW1 France
Member of American Expeditionary Forces to France, January to September 1918
Battle at Château-Thierry *Major battle/engagement/expedition for Jesse 2 June 1918
Battle at Belleau Woods Flanders Front
Verdun Sector
AEF Spring Drive of 1918

Indian Wars 1865-1898

Immediately after the Civil War, the United States Army was engaged in a series of small wars with the Red Man that was to last over thirty years. The Horse-Soldier as the Indians called them were in general hard-bitten breed of men, all but ignored in their own time, although they have since been much glorified in books and movies. Many of the troopers had been fighting each other just a short time before, wearing the blue or grey (American Civil War). The

Indian Wars were comprised of twelve distinct campaigns from 1865 to 1891, plus many engagements, up to 1898, varying from skirmishes to pitched battles. Hardly a three-month period passed without some expedition, yet the Indian Wars went comparatively unnoticed for some time. Congress did not recognize the fighting until March 1890, when it applied to Indian fighters the term "Veterans" in the same sense of the soldiers who had participated in a campaign against an armed enemy of the United States.

Indian Wars Medal

This award was not authorized by Congress until 11 January 1905, and was established by a War Department General order in 1907. The medal, designed by Frances D. Millet is bronze. On the obverse is a mounted Indian in a war bonnet carrying a spear. Above the horseman are the words "Indian Wars" and at the bottom is a buffalo skull at the center of a semi-circle of arrowheads. The reverse shows an eagle with wings, outspread, standing on a trophy composed of a cannon, crossed flag, spears, and Indian shield, a quiver, of arrows, a Cuban machete, and a Sulu Kris (Bolo knife). Below are the words "For Service". The whole is encircled by the words "United States Army" at the top and 13 stars below. The ribbon (suspension ribbon) is deep red with black stripes ¼ from each side. Originally, red with darker red edges, the ribbon was altered in 1917 to distinguish it from the French Legion of Honor

Note: The reverse design on the Indian Wars Medal is also used on the Puerto Rico Occupation Medal and the Philippine Campaign Medal, hence the machete and Bolo Knife on the design.

The Philippine Insurrection, 1899-1913

On 4 February 1899, Philippine patriots launched an assault against the United States occupation in Manila. The Americans embarked on a costly war against the Guerrillas. Which lasted officially until 4 July 1902. When a civil one superseded the Military Government. Hostilities however continued in some places until 1918.

Philippine-Campaign Medal

Authorized in 1905, this medal was awarded for service in the Philippines during the insurrection. It was also extended to cover actions in various parts of the island through 1913.The medal was designed by Frances D. Millet.

On the reverse is a coconut palm tree with a Roman Lamp at one side, symbolizing the enlightenment of the islands under American rule. On the other side of the tree are the scales of justice. Around the scene is a circle composed of the words Philippine Insurrection 1899. The reverse is the same as that of the Indian Wars Medal. The ribbon is blue flanked by broad stripes of red and narrow blue borders.

Spanish American War, 1898

On 15 February 1898, an explosion shook Havana Harbor, Cuba, and sank the United States Battleship Maine. Although the cause of the explosion was never indisputably determined, engaged Americans blamed the Spanish Government, and the United States declared war on Spain. The conflict lasted until 12 August, and in the peace treaty signed on 10 December, Spain gave up its claim to Cuba, Puerto Rico, the Philippines and Guam. The war was chiefly naval with fighting in both the Atlantic and Pacific Oceans. On 1 May the Atlantic Squadron, under the command of Commodore George Dewey, attacked and destroyed the Spanish fleet in Manila Bay, Philippines Islands.

Spanish War Service Medal

This medal sometimes called the National Guard Medal was authorized on 9 July 1918, for persons who served between 20 April 1898 and 11 April 1899, but were not eligible for the Spanish Campaign Medal. The obverse, designed by Colonel J.R.M Taylor, U.S. Army, shows a sheathed Roman Sword lying on a tablet inscribed for service in the Spanish War and surrounded by a wreath. The reverse, designed by Bailey, Banks and Biddle, has the United States coat of arms with a scroll below, all surrounded by a wreath displaying the Infantry, Artillery and Cavalry insignia. The ribbon is emerald green with two yellow stripes.

Army of Puerto Rico Occupational Medal

This was authorized in 1919 for service in Puerto Rico, 14 August to 10 December 1898. The obverse designed by the Army Heraldic Section, resembles the Spanish Campaign Medal. It has a similar castle with words, "Army of Puerto Rico", along the upper edge, and 1898 at the bottom, with a stalk of sugar cane at the right and a tobacco plant at the left. The reverse is the same as that of the Indian Wars Medal. The ribbon has a red stripe in the center, flanked by narrow yellow stripes, wide dark blue stripes, narrow red stripes.

Good Conduct Medal- Army

The Army Good Conduct Medal was authorized by executive order #8809 on 28 June 1941, awarded to enlisted men who have honorably completed three years of active duty subsequent to 26 August 1940, and who are recommended by their Commanding Officer for exemplary behavior, efficiency, and fidelity. Persons awarded this medal must have character and efficiency ratings of excellent or higher throughout the qualifying period, including time spent in attendance at service schools, and there must not be any conviction by court martial. Joseph Kiselewski designed the medal. On the obverse, an eagle with wings displayed and inverted, standing on a closed book, and has a Roman Sword. Encircling it is the inscription efficiency, honor, fidelity. The reverse has a five-pointed star, slightly above center, with a scroll beneath for the recipients' name. Above the star are the words for good, and below the scroll the word conduct. A wreath, formed of a Laurel Branch on the left and an oak branch on the right, surrounds the whole design. The ribbon, designed by Arthur E. Debois, is of scarlet moiré with three narrow stripes at either end. Only one Good Conduct Medal may be awarded to any one individual. For a second or subsequent award, a clasp is worn consisting of a bar 1 3/8 of an inch long and 1/8 inch wide, which had suspension loops.

Victory Medal WWI

This award was given to officers and enlisted men of the United States Armed Forces. These men had honorable record for active duty between 16 April 1917 and 11 November 1819 or for service with the Allied Expeditionary Force. (AEF) in Europe, Russia, 11 November 1918 to 1 April 1920. Designed by James E. Fraser. A bronze medal with the same ribbon as for the British Victory Medal. On the obverse is the winged figure of victory, while the reverse has the shield of the United States with the letters "U.S." and the names of the associated powers. A unique feature of this medal was the adoption of clasps to be worn on the suspension ribbon. The Army adopted thirteen battle clasps to indicate participation in a major campaign, and a defensive sector clasp. The following clasps were issued:

Cambrai, Somme Defensive, Lys, Aisne, Montdidier-Noyon, Champagne-Marne,

Aisne-Marne, Somme Offensive, Aisne, Ypres-Lys, St. Mihel, Meuse-Argonne,

Vittorio-Veneo

All of the above were major operations, and with another clasp, Defensive Sector, are indicated by a small bronze star on the ribbon when it is worn alone. Five service clasps, France, Italy, Siberia, Russia and England were also authorized for the Army, but not awarded to persons entitled to battle clasps, and do not carry the right to wear the bronze star on the service ribbon. The small Silver Star originally worn on the Victory ribbon, to indicate a citation for gallantry in action was later replaced by the separate Silver Star medal.

Chickenhawk

Indian name Eskehnadestah (known as chicken)
Army Serial Number: R 1140061
Organization: Indian Scouts
Born: 1 January 1875
Retired: 12 February 1924
Service: 31 years 1 month

Enlisted: 3 July 1893
Discharged: 3 January 1895
Grade: Private

Enlisted: 4 January 1895
Discharged: 3 January 1898
Grade: Private

Enlisted: 4 January 1898
Discharged: 3 January 1901
Grade: Private

Enlisted: 4 January 1901
Discharged: 3 January 1904
Grade: Corporal

Enlisted: 4 January
Discharged 3 January 1907
Grade: Sergeant

Enlisted: 4 January 1907
Discharged: 3 January 1910
Grade: 1st Sergeant

Enlisted: 4 January 1910
Discharged: 3 January 1913
Grade: Private

Enlisted: 4 January 1913
Discharged: 3 January 1917
Grade: 1st Sergeant

Enlisted: 4 January 1917
Discharged: 2 January 1920
Grade: 1st Sergeant

Enlisted: 3 January 1920
Discharged: 2 January 1923
Grade: Sergeant

Enlisted 3 January
Discharged: 12 February 1924
Grade: Master Sergeant

Jesse's words At Fort Apache, I had an excellent relationship with Chicken. We hunted together for a few days on Willow Creek, a branch of the Black River. He was on a manhunt with me after a Trooper, who went AWOL, and was hiking south towards Globe. The Scouts successfully tracked the soldier. We apprehended him near the lower White River Bridge, close to Tom Wanslee's Trading Store. In addition to those trips together, there were many other routine contacts at the fort. He, of course did not handle the First Sergeant's paperwork that was done by a white soldier of the Quartermaster Detachment but I always gave him orders and other matters regarding the Scouts for him to execute and pass along. He was always a good leader, and a highly respected man at the fort. Most of the officers, who had soldiered with Chicken, spoke in the highest terms about the qualities of this man. However, the comments of the book "As a Cavalryman remembers" contended that Chicken was a Morse, a bad tempered Indian. It is my surmise that Rodney did not like the Apaches, and they naturally reacted accordingly. The Old Scout died at White River Agency Hospital on 3 February 1955. His survivors were two sons, six daughters' twenty-seven grandchildren and two great-grandchildren. He was buried in the cemetery at the Agency Post.

Skippyjack

Indian name: Eskipbygojo
Army Serial Number: R 1140072
Organization: Indian Scouts
Born: 1 January 1870
Died: Date unknown

Enlisted: 1 July 1892
Discharged: 31 December 1892
Grade: Private

Enlisted: 1 January 1893
Discharged: 30 June 1893
Grade: Private

Enlisted: 1 July 1893
Enlisted: 31 December 1893
Grade: Private

Enlisted: 1 January
Discharged: 30 June 1894
Grade: Private

Enlisted: 4 July 1894
Discharged: 3 January 1895
Grade: Private

Enlisted: 4 January 1895
Discharged: 3 January 1904
Grade: Private

Enlisted: 1 January 1913
Discharged: 31 December 1916
Grade: Private

Enlisted: 1 January 1917
Discharged: 2 January 1920
Grade: Private

Enlisted: 3 January 1920
Discharged: 3 January 1923
Grade: Private

Enlisted: 3 January 1923
Discharged: 2 January 1926
Grade: Private

Enlisted: 3 January 1926
Discharged: 2 January 1929
Grade: Private

Eskipbygojo had served twenty-seven years and six months upon the expiration of his last enlistment, which was two and a half years short of the requirement for retirement pay. It is hoped that the officer in command of the detachment used all efforts to persuade the Apache to serve the few years in order to earn the continued pay. However, it is also realized that when an Indian wanted to return to his home reservation, argument and influence counts for little in changing the fixed idea. Many a white soldier, when the thirty-year period was effective, failed by a few years, even a few weeks to complete his service in order to retire. Perhaps a psychologist can explain the strange actions by some of the old soldiers. Eskipbygojo included, which caused them to refuse to re-enlist, go AWOL or desert near the end, a few even commit suicide.

General Interest

Jesse was no angel as you can tell when you read Chapter One. The following general remarks will help clarify things that happened in his military career. Our family weaves some of the comments in, mostly of my Aunt Peggy (deceased) and my father. I might add that at the start of this project, my father was in contact with Lori Davisson of the Arizona Historical Society. Our family has since learned of her passing and our family thanks her for her time and friendship. We are sure she is missed greatly.

In the military unauthorized absences is an absence of less than thirty days. The common term used is AWOL (absent without leave) any absence over thirty days is considered desertion. Jesse was AWOL on two occasions- 30 October 1912 to 1 November 1912 and 9 November 1913 to 11 November 1913. Usually in cases of AWOL, there is a minor punishment. In addition to the punishment the time, AWOL must be made up by serving the number of days AWOL as an extension to the current enlistment period. It appears Jesse was punished for being AWOL by a reduction in grade and probably a fine. A fine, reduction in grade and confinement (jail), could have punished him. He enlisted on 19 February 1911, and was discharged on February 23 1914. From this information, you can tell he had enlisted for three years in 1911. He should have been discharged on 19 February 1914, but was discharged on February 23 1914, having served for extra days for the four days he was AWOL during that enlistment.

He was marked a deserter from 20 April 1904 to 27 May 1904. His next enlistment was 23 January 1908 under the name of John R. Day. There is a four-year gap between the times he was marked as a deserter. When he next enlisted, it seems he was caught by the military, and sentenced to jail for his desertion.

He received a dishonorable discharge 19 March 1898. His enlistment period was 3 May 1896 to 19 March 1898. Evidently he did something wrong.

Our guess is he did this sometime in February or March 1898. He could have been Court Martial or discharged from the military, it appears he was just discharged. It was told at this time that Jesse was stripped naked and was made to run through the town at Fort Apache, Arizona. This story was told to my father by his father, but not what he did to warrant the dishonorable discharge.

Having enlisted in 1893 under the name of Henry C. Hays, and remained known under that name up to his dishonorable discharge in 1898. After his dishonorable discharge at Fort Apache, he joined the Army Signal Corps April/May of 1898 to June/July 1898. He got into some type of a disagreement with the Sergeant and left the Army Signal Corps. He ended up with the First City Troop of Philadelphia July 1898. We know he enlisted under a false name and volunteered as a horseman and the City Troop Cook during the Spanish American War. Through research, we found out, he was on the U.S Transport Massachusetts that ran aground in a coral reef off the coast of Puerto Rico 3 August 1898. At the end of the Spanish American War, he was placed on the U.S. Transport heading back to the United States. The Mississippi Transport docked in Jersey City 10 September 1898. From there he took a train back to Philadelphia. He remained in the city until 1899. His next enlistment was under his birth name Jesse C. Davisson in 1899 until 1902. His next enlistment was April 20, 1904 to 27 May 1904, when he deserted, what name is anybody's guess. He next enlisted under the name John R. Day in 1908 until January 1911.

Enlisted in February 1911, under the name John R. Day until February 1914. He then enlisted under his birth name Jesse C. Davisson in March 1914 until his discharge in 1918. Jesse used different names when enlisting to enable him to get back in the military. He also used different names when he was a civilian. While in Puerto Rico, he was called Jack.

Jesse enlisted under the name Henry C. Hays on 26 January 1898 (my father's birthday) must be some connection there as Jesse and my father are the only ones in our family to serve in the military. He enlisted in Camden, New Jersey. He was initially turned down at the Fairmont Recruiting Station in Philadelphia; he failed because of his feet. He then crossed the Delaware to Camden after one of the Sergeants at the Philadelphia office suggested he try there.

His pay would have been $13.00 a month. Both his pay and living conditions would improve, but not by much. In putting this book together, I used the diary he wrote, along with his discharge papers and notes he jotted down on loose paper. He did not write about all the places he had been to Jesse's hobby were keeping scrapbooks. One note of interest he made was on a newspaper photo showing WW2 troops in a landing craft. On the clipping, he wrote: Third man in the middle Corporal Bobby (Dad's brother, my uncle). It certainly looked like my Uncle Bob. One note he made was on a photo of military awards. He wrote these are the medals I received. He had an argument with the U.S. Government about one of the awards he thought he should have received.

Another interesting notation was besides a clipping of a horse named Comanche. Comanche was the horse of Captain Myles Keogh. Captain Keogh was killed at the Battle of Little Bighorn (General Custer's last fight). Comanche was the only living thing that survived the battle. Jesse wrote he would steal hairs from Comanche's tail, and have an Indian weave the hairs into a charm for him. Comanche died in 1891 at Fort Riley, Kansas. Jesse did not enlist in the Army until 1893. Another note was beside a photo of a horse drawn trolley car in Philadelphia. My grandfather said Jesse never drove a horse drawn trolley car. Jesse seemed to tell little lies at times.

In 1921he enrolled in elementary education classes at Temple University in Philadelphia, Pa. He started in January 1921 and should have completed the course in August 1921. He studied English and arithmetic in January and February. Then quit the course.

Jesse was first trained at Jefferson Barracks, St. Louis, Missouri, where he received his basic military training. From there he was stationed in Texas, Arizona, New Mexico, Utah, New York, Puerto Rico, Hawaii, Philippine Islands and France. I have given a brief history of the paces he was stationed at in the United States with the exception of one post. Camp J.D.Mann, Texas. In all the research I have done, I could not find mention of a Camp J.D.Mann. It is possible the camp was known by the name of the commander, as this was not uncommon during these times. Jesse said the camp was eighty miles down on the Rio Grande River, having got off the train in Laredo, Texas. Two posts fit this description, Fort Ringwold and Fort Brown. On a scrap piece of paper,

he noted he was stationed at Fort Brown. He also mentions two places of interest, Cibicue Creek and San Carlos. Cibcue Creek, Arizona was where he was
sent because an Indian Chief was killed by two white men and he faced hostile
Indians the entire time he was there, At San Carlos, New Mexico he joined up
with others to go into the Black Mountains of Arizona to hunt for Indians who
left the reservation.

It has been told to me, by my father. That my Grandfather, (Dad's father)
had a very soft spot in his heart for my Great-Grandfather Jesse. My father
gathered this information from conversations they had about him before my
grandfather passed on. My father (Jesse's grandson) and I write both these pages
in the General Interest.

A Philadelphian family

After Jesse was discharged for the final time from the Army, he went and worked for the family business in Philadelphia. My father (Jesse's grandson) writes this part of the book.

When Jesse first signed up in 1893 my grandmother tracked Jesse down in three years and obtained a divorce. After his final discharge, he and Elizabeth remarried. Jesse went to work in the ice and coal family business mainly taking care of Bill and Bill the two horses. The company's name was Northend Ice and Coal Delivery Company in Philadelphia. It was located at 527 Diamond Street. Horse and wagon made deliveries; two horses pulled the wagon. One was named Bill and the other one was Bill. When I asked why two horses with the same name were pulling I was told, "When you say Giddap Bill." both horses would pull at the same time.

My Aunt Katie married an Englishman named George Kershaw. Jesse did not care at all for Mr. Kershaw, as Mr. Kershaw did not do any work. If there were any work to be done around the stable or yard George would say, "Time for a spot of tea." Jesse would shout, "Son of a bitch limey never does anything around here but have a cup of tea!"

My father told me Bill and Bill would stamp on Jesse's feet quite a bit, and did a pretty good job on them. Jesse and Elizabeth would sit out in the yard on Diamond Street as they were living there with my Uncle Joe. My sister, brother, and I liked going around to Diamond Street (one block away from our house) and run into the yard. Jesse would shout, "Damn kids keep away from my feet, keep away from my feet!"

I remember Jesse coming to our house, usually none the worse, for the beer he drank in Nicky Kuhn's Saloon. The saloon was around the corner from our house at Fairhill Street and Susquehanna Avenue. When Jesse came in, he always wanted tomato soup to eat. My father would get very angry with him as Jesse was laughing and joking all the time, demanding his tomato soup. I cannot remember the things he said, but my sister (Peg), and brother (Bob) and I used to laugh at him. Laughing at him seemed to egg him on. My sister told me the reason my father was so angry with Jesse was that Jesse probably had been drinking for the past few days and had not gone home. My father would have to take Jesse home to face my grandmother and try to calm the waters.

While eating his favorite tomato soup he would talk with his hands waving all about with a spoon in his one hand. He would end up splashing the soup all around making a mess. My mother (Irma) did not say much, but she also calmed the waters between my father and Jesse during his visits.

Due to his being gassed in WWI, he had a chest problem, and in the early forties it got the better of him. He was confined to bed. He was placed at my Uncle Joe's bedroom. On the second floor of the house on Diamond Street. My mother made my sister, brother, and me go around and visit Jesse. Not all of the children went at the same time. Seems to me I spent quite a bit of time visiting Jesse. While there he would tell me about all the places he visited, and what he did. Being young, I did not pay too much attention to what he telling me. I just wanted to go outside and play. Eventually he would fall asleep, or so you thought. As soon as you tried to sneak out of the bedroom he would grab his cane, and reach out, and hook it around your neck, and drag you back to his bedside. I only wished I would have been a little older and remembered what he was telling me.

Due to his chest problem, he was admitted to the Philadelphia Navy Hospital. I remember going to the Navy Hospital with my parents, sister, brother, and grandmother. Since I was too young to be allowed in as a visitor, I had to stay outside. My brother was placed in charge of me. At the entrance to the hospital was a military guard carrying a rifle. My brother told me if I crossed a yellow drawn at the entrance the guard will shoot me. Next thing I knew he pushed me across the line drawn. All I could think was that I would be shot for visiting my grandfather, and I wish I was nicer to him at my Uncle Joe's house. I shut my eyes and all I heard were my brother and the guard laughing.

One of Jesse's favorite ways to make me upset would be to tell me, "Since you were a bad boy, I am going to take you to the cathouse." I asked my father what a cathouse was. Jesse said, "It's a place where they beat you with a cat o' nine tails!" Every time he would say this to me my grandmother would say, "Jesse stop it!" When I reflect back on what he said and the way he would laugh when he said it, I do not think my father and Jesse were talking about the same cathouse.

First City Troop, Philadelphia City Cavalry
Pennsylvania Volunteer Cavalry

The First City Troop Cavalry, which has been in the National Guard of Pennsylvania since the organization of the Guard, is the oldest military organization in continuous active military service in the United States, dating back to November 17, 1774. In compliance with General Orders No. 7, Headquarters National Guard of Pennsylvania, this troop assembled at their Armory at 5 o'clock A.M., April 28 1898 and at 5:45 A.M., left the Armory mounted, armed and fully equipped, and embarked on the cars for Mount Gretna, Pa., for the purpose of volunteering in the United States service during the war with Spain. They arrived at Mount Gretna Pa., at 2:30 P.M., April 28 1898, and on May 7 the troop was mustered into the United States Volunteer service, as the First City Troop, Philadelphia City Cavalry, Pennsylvania Volunteer Cavalry, and consisted of three officers and sixty enlisted men, every officer and enlisted man having volunteered. The troop remained at Mount Gretna until July 7, during which time the War Department directed that the troop be recruited to enlist 100 men. On June 17th, Captain Groome, as the senior officer of Volunteer Cavalry of Pennsylvania, formed the First Troop, the Sheridan Troop, and the Governor's Troop into a squadron and assumed command thereof. On July 17, under orders from the War Department the squadron proceeded to Camp Alger, Virginia, arriving July 8th, and was attached to Headquarters Second Army Corps. At this time, the First Troop had ninety-eight men on the rolls. While at Camp Alger, Government arms and equipments were issued and the troop arms and equipments were returned to Philadelphia. Under orders from the War Department, the Squadron left Camp Alger on the evening of July 24 and proceeded to Newport News, Virginia, arriving on the evening of July 25, when the first City Troop received orders to proceed to Porto Rico. It embarked on the United States transport "Massachusetts," which sailed a noon on

July 28, 1898; three officers and ninety-nine enlisted men, 105 horses and 16 draft mules, and four drivers. On August 3rd, the transport arrived off Ponce, Porto Rico, and ran aground on a coral reef, delaying the disembarkation, but the troop, with their arms and equipments, were taken off in lighters, landed at the Playa of Ponce, and bivouacked about the Cathedral Virgin del Carmen, being the first cavalry landed at Porto Rico. The following morning the work of lightering the horses commenced and was not completed until August 6th

The Troop received orders to report to Major General Brooke at Guayama, left Playa of Ponce, August 8th and went into camp about ten miles beyond Ponce. August 9th they joined troop "H," of the 6th U.S. Cavalry, and acting as an escort to the Hospital train, signal service, headquarters horses and wagon train, marched to Arroyo, arriving there August 10th, and reported to Major General Brooke, and went into camp about one mile from General Brooke's Headquarters. On the evening of August 12th orders were received from General Brooke for the First City Troop Cavalry and Troop "H" Six United States Cavalry, "To be on the road to Guayama at 6:20 A.M. the following morning," The two Troops proceeded to Guayama the following morning, August 13 and report to General Brooke about two miles beyond the town on the road to Cayey, where they were ordered to take position on the right of the line formed to attack to Spanish entrenchments ay Aybonito. About 11 o'clock A.M., just as the artillery were ready to commence firing, General Brookes received orders to suspend all military operations as a Peace Protocol had been signed. The two Troops were ordered to return to Guayama and go into camp. On the 14th of August, a cavalry outpost was established, two miles beyond the infantry outpost, on the road to Aybonita, overlooking the enemy's works on the mountainside, and the two troops alternated in furnishing the guard. Captain Scott, Sixth U.S. Cavalry, having joined "H" Troop, relieved Captain Groome of the command of the two troops, and assumed command. On August 25th the First Troop received orders to return to Ponce, and take transport for the United States and arrived at Ponce August 26th and went into camp. On September 2nd the troop embarked on the U.S. transport "Mississippi, which sailed for New York at 6 o'clock A.M., September 3rd, arriving at Jersey City 7:25 P.M. September 10th. The Troop was furloughed for sixty days, and on November 21, 1898, was mustered out of the service of the United States.

Jesse cut this out of a paper and put it in one of his many scrapbooks.

Picture taken by Fowler Studios in Philadelphia. Age 24.

Picture was most likely taken by a Fort Photographer. June 1894. At Eagle Pass, Texas.

Crossed swords are the insignia of the Cavalry. "G" stands for Troop G and the "7" for the Cavalry

Inscription on lower right: Jesse on his horse King. In the Black Canyon, Arizona Territory. Inscriptions at the top of the photo read: I only went with them (cowboys) on a roundup. I had lots of fun and my eats for nothing. I could never throw a rope or get a cow. I used to try a lot, but could never get one. I was only a bluff as a Cowboy.

Inscription at the left hand side: But ride em boys ride. I could do that. That is if they would not Crawfish turn their heads down right or left and try to throw you over their shoulders or head.

Troop G 7th Cavalry. Camp Eagle Pass, Texas. Jesse is holding the flag.

Jesse is standing top far left. He wrote at the bottom by the feet area: Standing first from left is me. May 1892

Photo of three Apache Indians believed to be White Mountain Apaches. On left the names appears to be TA-HIL-Sette. On the right PA-HIL-Sette and the middle MA-HIL-Sette. Picture was taken by D.A. Markey. Fort Grant, Arizona.

Troop G, 7th Cavalry, 16 November 1895 at Fort Apache, Arizona. Man at far left holding the flag is Jesse. Post Photographer was George A. Brown.

3. 7TH CAVALRY ARRIVING AT FORT APACHE. JESSE IS CARRY
US. USING THE PONY AS A STARTING POINT, COUNT BACK TH

Troop G 7th Cavalry arriving at Fort Apache. Jesse is carrying the flag. Using the pony as a starting point. Count back three white horses on the outside row. Jesse is in between the second and third white horse on the inside row. He has a white spot on his shoulder. It does appear that the man behind Jesse with the cap, is carrying the flag. Jesse wrote that is was not him carrying the flag that day. Jesse came from Fort Apache to meet the Troop.

7th Cavalry Trumpeter Corps, standing in center is Chief Trumpeter Harding. Chief Trumpeter Harding played taps over the grave of General Sheridan at St, Louis Missouri.

Troop G 7th Cavalry at Fort Riley Kansas. Jesse wrote on picture: One of the men on the bottom row robbed the Paymaster of six-thousand dollars. He stole it out of the Guard House at Fort Clark, Texas. He is now is prison serving 5 years. I am not in this photo Notice the stile caps we wore in those days. * Jesse did not indicate what man on the bottom row stole the money. However the man in the middle has very shifty eyes. My father has the original of this photo.

Picture Information

Pictures of Jesse can be purchased through The Arizona Historical Society. Under the following: Jesse C. Davisson Troop G 7th Cavalry, Tucson Stacks, Call # PC 203 Troop G 7th Cavalry, Fort Apache, United States Army.